· LONELINESS AND LOVE ·

L. VANDER KERKEN, S.J.

Loneliness and Love

•

Translated with a Foreword
by J. Donceel, S.J.

SHEED & WARD • NEW YORK

LIBRARY OF CONGRESS CATALOG CARD NUMBER
67–14817

IMPRIMI POTEST:
ROBERT A. MITCHELL, S.J.
OCTOBER 7, 1966

NIHIL OBSTAT:
LEO J. STEADY, PH.D., S.T.D.
CENSOR LIBRORUM

IMPRIMATUR:
✠ROBERT F. JOYCE
BISHOP OF BURLINGTON
NOVEMBER 7, 1966

THE NIHIL OBSTAT AND IMPRIMATUR ARE OFFICIAL
DECLARATIONS THAT A BOOK OR PAMPHLET IS CON-
SIDERED TO BE FREE OF DOCTRINAL OR MORAL ER-
ROR. NO IMPLICATION IS CONTAINED THEREIN THAT
THOSE WHO HAVE GRANTED THE NIHIL OBSTAT AND
IMPRIMATUR AGREE WITH THE CONTENTS, OPINIONS
OR STATEMENTS EXPRESSED.

· Foreword ·

ANOTHER BOOK ABOUT LOVE. But after Scheler, Rousselot, Nygren, Marcel, Nédoncelle, and, closer to home, von Hildebrand, Johann, and Wilhelmsen, have we not had our fill? This might be true unless there are topics about which it is impossible to say or read enough. Love appears to be one of the realities that are of their very nature inexhaustible.

Father Vander Kerken is especially equipped to deal with the perennial subject. He belongs to that group of Flemish thinkers whose profound and original writings have made a lasting contribution to Christian philosophy and theology. His books on Esthetics, Happiness, and Basic Moral Attitudes have already been well received in the Low Countries. The present study is a reworked version of an article that originally appeared in the review *Bijdragen* in 1946. Accommodating himself to the desires of the many readers who asked that the article be made available in the form of a booklet, the author, after some twenty years of reflection, has considerably amplified and refined his earlier statement. *Loneliness and Love,* therefore, is the mature work of an established scholar.

As with St. Augustine's analysis of time, everyone knows what love is until he is asked to define it. It is always difficult to translate our unverbalized experience into words, and this is especially true of love: it is easier to experience and live it than to analyze or define it. In everyday language we use the verb "to love" in many contexts. It may refer to our favorite food, a walk in the woods, the music of Bach, country, friends, family, and God. We simply do not have a vocabulary that can accommodate itself to every nuance, although the English language provides us with the verb "to like," which stands for a less intense kind of loving.

In any case, it is evident that there is quite a difference between the way we love or like lobster or a college degree and the way we like our friends and love our children. In the former instances our immediate aim is to get hold of some object as a means of enjoyment or enrichment; whereas, where people are concerned, unless we are consummate egoists, we are attracted by the person. We do not merely desire the company of this person as a means of enjoyment or enrichment, but we treat him as an end. If we desire him to prosper and be happy, it is not for our own advantage. That is why Maurice Nédoncelle defines love as *une volonté de promotion*.

Yet even in this case there can be a lurking element of selfishness. Perhaps we desire the company and attention of the person we love not simply for his own good but because we also derive pleasure and happiness from them. Does this imply that, to some extent, all love is selfish?

St. Thomas was aware of the problem when he took over from Aristotle the distinction between love of benevolence: *amor benevolentiae* (also known as love of friendship: *amor amicitiae*) and love of desire: *amor concupiscentiae*. The latter is motivated by some attractive quality discovered in the beloved person which we desire to enjoy and share; the former goes out to the person himself, to his very selfhood. Thus, the question amounts to asking whether all love of friendship is ultimately love of desire.

St. Thomas and those who adopted the *physical* conception of love defended the affirmative position. They admitted that all love was based ultimately on love of self, without admitting, however, that this meant that all love was selfish. Love is rooted in appetite, and all appetite, even the most sublime, implies that the subject strives primarily for his own good and perfection. Thus, the love of self becomes the soul of every love, while love of the other is secondary, deriving from the primary love of self. When it is extended to the other because he resembles me, it is because I recover myself in him.

On the other hand, the *ecstatic* conception of love, as defended especially by the Franciscan doctors, held that love's perfection increases as the loving subject steps more completely outside himself and more fully forgets himself. Real love is not a mere prolongation of the subject's basic appetite; it transcends it and frequently goes against it. In real love the subject loses himself.

Medieval philosophers were fond of setting the difference in sharp contrast by asking whether a man should be willing to give up his own eternal happiness out of love for God. The proponents of the physical conception answered by arguing that since one cannot do this, one should not. The ecstatics replied: Granting the hypothesis and assuming that the man of perfect love were faced with such a choice, he would have to surrender his own eternal happiness out of a motive of pure and heroic love of God.

At first blush the heroic answer might seem to correspond better with the idealized picture which most people like to entertain about pure love. But a few moments' reflection will uncover an insuperable practical difficulty against it: the one who, out of love of God, would try to make the supreme sacrifice of his own eternal happiness would thereby perform an act of such superhuman love that it is hard to see how he could ever be separated from the Supreme Love who is also the Supreme Beatitude. The very attempt to perform such an act of heroic love would be self-defeating and only result in profiting and adding to the stature of man's higher self. Man never takes better care of himself than when he tries utterly to forget himself.

In speaking of the self we must distinguish between a lower self of drives and instincts and a higher spiritual self: the former should occasionally not only be forgotten; it should even be given up and sacrificed. The latter, on the other hand, while it may and should be forgotten or overlooked, can never really be surrendered even in the most selfless love. Nothing "profits" this spiritual self more than what is called unselfish love, a love that grows in perfection in direct proportion to the extent that it forgets and more fully ignores the unavoidable advantages accruing to the loving subject from this kind of love. In other words, we may no more apply the term *selfish* to a love that brings this sort of benefit to the spiritual self than we can apply it to the infinite love with which God necessarily loves himself.

So it is without apologies that the author espouses the physical conception of love when he writes:

> Every token of affection involves some appropriation of the person to whom affection is shown. In this sense every *love of benevolence* is wrapped in a *love of concupiscence,* because the very granting of affection remains the *possession* of the one who grants it. Man is unable to give himself unreservedly. Even when the utmost unselfishness is achieved, the selflessness of love will return as his *own* perfection to the one who practices it. This means a defect, not in the perfection itself, but in the fact that it can never be experienced in such a way that it becomes identically the perfection of the one loved. It is not necessary to strive towards such an ideal, for its realization can only be deceptive; an inhuman fusion of two beings is confused with absolute love.[1]

None of this detracts from the greatness of spiritual love. Father Vander Kerken's great friend and colleague, Pierre Scheuer, has treated this topic in a few

1. P. 51.

short sentences that penetrate to the heart of the problem.[2] He points out that man is spirit in matter and that the point of view of spirit, *even of a finite spirit in matter,* is absolute. Hence, as things appear to a finite intellect, so they are absolutely in themselves. When with my spiritual will I love what is good for my spiritual self, I love identically what is *absolutely good in itself.*

At first glance the assertion that what is good for me as a spirit is absolutely good may appear questionable and utterly dogmatic. But any attempt to deny it is self-refuting. So at the risk of irritating the reader, I would ask his indulgence for just one paragraph in order to show why this is the case.

Whoever denies that reality as known by a spirit is identically reality as it is in itself affirms this statement in his very denial. What he has done is to reject the equality I have asserted between reality as it is in itself and reality as it is in my spirit. But the moment he insists that his rejection of equality has validity, he simultaneously asserts that the lack of equality which his intellect perceives corresponds to a lack of equality in reality. So he affirms that, as things are in his spirit, so they are in reality. In denying my statement about equality, all he does is replace it with his own state-

2. See in Daniel J. Shine, S.J., *An Interior Metaphysics* (Weston, Mass.: Weston College Press), p. 91.

ment which implicitly but necessarily affirms the very equality he denies—and he does this in the very act of denial. Therefore, his statement of denial is self-contradictory.

Hence, what is true for me as a spirit is absolutely true. No doubt, we have been talking about goodness, but since ontological truth and ontological goodness are "convertible," what is good for me as a spirit is absolutely good; or, to return to our point of departure, disinterested human love is absolute love; it cannot be relative or selfish.

It is somewhat distressing to have to introduce this kind of abstruse reasoning into a Preface for a book that is remarkably free from anything of the sort. For if it does contain a few short passages that require closer reading, they are lost among the many pages containing some of the deepest and most beautiful paragraphs that, to my knowledge, have ever been written on loneliness, love, and friendship. But perhaps it may not have been out of place to try to show that even metaphysics supports the spontaneous reverence which the human mind harbors for truly disinterested love.   J. DONCEEL, S.J.

· Preface ·

IT HAS BECOME FASHIONABLE in modern literature to speak disparagingly of man. Unfortunately this criticism is not always unfounded. Has he not demonstrated that he is capable of the worst crimes? And can we conceive of any kind of evil which men have not done, or at least have not wanted to do? Some philosophers, turning this over in their minds, have become pessimistic; they have even begun to call man's capacity for good into question. We wonder whether this is the best way of penetrating into the secret depths of man's nature. There is another side, and we would like to emphasize this other side. The question is which of the two is the stronger. We can, perhaps, answer that question at once. For is not the slightest goodness discovered in man much more significant than all the evil which contradicts it? Does it not immediately tell us much more about man's real nature than all the wrongs and ugliness which are so glibly emphasized?

We shall look for this goodness and see how it manifests itself in the relations between persons. These relations reach their peak in love and friendship. Hence these two wonderful realities, which are the source of so much joy in human experience, will occupy our attention.

· Contents ·

Contents

• LONELINESS AND LOVE •

· CHAPTER I ·

The Other Person

LIKE ALL OTHER RELATIONS between human beings, love and friendship are possible only on the basis of a bond which is one of the very elements of man's nature. Although this bond develops fully only in the association between persons, it is a prerequisite of such association. Human relations would be impossible if man were not, by his very nature, a social being. Therefore every study of human relations will have to start from an insight into the nature of this sociality. Partial studies may offer interesting descriptions, but they are always in danger of overlooking the real meaning of the phenomena, or at least of bogging down in psychological considerations.

5

It is one of the merits of modern philosophy that it has seriously studied the problem of sociality. True, earlier philosophers recognized that man was a social being. Aristotle called him a *"zoon politicon,"* a being destined to live in society. But it is undeniable that in the past there was a strong tendency to consider man's propensity for social life, if not as a merely extrinsic feature, at least as only a secondary characteristic. There were even philosophers, such as Jean-Jacques Rousseau and Thomas Hobbes, who simply denied man's social nature and considered society to be only the necessary means for individuals to survive in the struggle for life. Such a conception is diametrically opposed to the modern view. At least, to be precise, this is true so far as the philosophers are concerned. For the older ideas have not yet completely disappeared. There are still thinkers who look on mankind as a mere sum of individuals (one plus one plus one plus one. . . .), trying to survive amidst competition and strife. But in philosophy such a conception is dead. In modern philosophy sociality is not a *more or less* essential feature of man, man is not a being who, along with other qualities, possesses that of being social. For philosophy man is simply and wholly a social being. This view is the right one, and we must find out what it really implies.

To this end we must enter human consciousness

and discover how man experiences his sociality. Surprisingly, this experience begins at the first moment when the human being realizes that he exists as self-consciousness. Hegel has skillfully described this process in his *Phenomenology of Mind*, under precisely the aspect which interests us. We cannot do better than to follow him briefly in this description.

Hegel starts with a dialectical analysis of the first phases of human knowledge: sensation, perception and understanding. In all these "moments" consciousness is still full of the "other." Even considered as intellectual knowledge, it is still wholly engaged with the ordering of this "other," external to itself, according to species and laws. Consciousness is not aware that all this keeps it, as it were, outside itself. Nevertheless, according to Hegel, the understanding has entered into some kind of "conversation with itself" without being aware of it. Then, all at once, it grasps this multiple intellectual activity as one whole, thus seeing "intellectual knowledge" for what it really is, and understanding it as its own operation. This allows consciousness to emerge, to some extent, from its involvement in the outside world. It so to speak disentangles itself from this world and comes to itself. Whereas, up to this point, knowledge has been entirely dominated by that which is "other than consciousness," now it effects a return to consciousness itself. It becomes an internal mirroring of consciousness in itself and enters into *"das einheimische Reich der Wahrheit"* (the native land of truth).[1]

Thus, according to Hegel, self-consciousness results from a transcendence of the other. The mind may be greatly tempted to leave all this other behind and look for truth only within itself. But the first effort in this direction shows the temptation up as an illusion. Detached from the outside world, which has so far been the object of knowledge, self-consciousness falls back into the sterile tautology of a *"Ich bin Ich"* (I am I).[2] Such is the condition of human consciousness, that it must meet its inner truth outside itself, if it wants to possess it really as an objective content. This does not mean that self-consciousness possesses no real content, or that man's interiority is nothing but a point of reference for the outside world. It means only that man's self-consciousness is unable to grasp its own truth when it locks itself up in itself and refuses to contemplate the other. Scholastic philosophy as well has always held that the intellect—even though essentially transcending sense knowledge—can reach its own truth only in connection with this sense knowledge. At any rate, it is evident that at the start of its development self-consciousness is only potential self-consciousness. It stands, as it were, only on the threshold of itself. It must fully become what it already is as a pos-

8

sibility, real self-consciousness. Its whole truth is still to be attained. What has been reached thus far is only the discovery of it as a real possibility, but as a result its conquest is not far off.

Human consciousness, although it has discovered itself as self-consciousness, has not ceased to be aware of things external to it. It has not given up its essential extraversion. In the process of becoming aware of itself, it will always remain dependent on the other. "There is nothing in the intellect that has not first been"—or, if you like, "that is not at the same time" —"in the senses" applies also to self-consciousness. This means that in order to reach the knowledge of itself, self-consciousness, too, will somehow have to contemplate this "self" in the other. But how can self-consciousness discover itself in the other, unless the other too reveals itself as a real selfhood, unless it presents some content which corresponds adequately to that of self-consciousness? How can a human being reach the objective knowledge of himself if this "being-himself" is not given to him as the visible spectacle of another "himself"?

Hegel considers this a *conditio sine qua non*, a necessary condition, but, as we must add at once, a condition which will necessarily be fulfilled, for the simple reason that human beings do in fact reach effective self-consciousness. It is not necessary to make sure dialectically that this condition will be fulfilled. For an unprejudiced phenomenological examination will at once make evident that the process of becoming self-conscious always occurs in function of another self-consciousness. Dialectics will merely explain why this is true, and why it has to happen that way.

Therefore we may say with Hegel: self-consciousness is standing before another self-consciousness. Or, in other words, self-consciousness *"ist ausser sich gekommen,"* it has come outside itself,[3] outside its empty and tautological enclosure, and discovered its essence before itself as an objective datum. But this still does not take us very far. The only gain is that what was at first only a subjective possibility of effectively becoming self-conscious has discovered a foundation in objective exteriority, thus becoming an objective possibility. All the conditions required for real self-consciousness are now fulfilled, but the actual process of becoming truly and clearly self-conscious has not yet taken place. For the brute fact of looking at a being which is really "another human being" is not yet real knowledge, as long as it does not become an acknowledgment of that human being as a human being. It is but a material nearness, not yet a true presence. And as long as man does not acknowledge the other as another human being, he cannot become aware of his own being human, since, as we have seen, self-knowledge is wholly tied to the fact of acknowledging the other person. Therefore we must examine this process of acknowledging.

We must not conceive it as something which happens all at once, suddenly putting man in full possession of himself, thus opening wide for him the world of human relations. Nobody has ever passed through such an experience. It is rather a long-drawn-out experience, slowly maturing, developing with life, and, to a great extent, giving each life its content. It is an experience which, starting almost imperceptibly with existence itself, emerges sooner or later into clear consciousness and reaches its highest form in the various kinds of affection and love.

An important aspect of this process of acknowledging is that the process of reaching self-consciousness in the light of another self-consciousness can never be one-sided. It is necessarily reciprocal. Man cannot discover himself in the other if the other does not meet him halfway in a complementary voyage of discovery. Failing this, and should the other person remain shut up in himself, this person would be for him but a living thing, an object of intellectual knowledge, by no means the living mirror which can reflect his own humanness.

When we use the word "mirror," we simply translate into ordinary English what philosophy means by the scholarly term "reflection." Self-consciousness is called reflective consciousness; it casts its light back upon itself; it shines inwardly, thus coming to know itself; in short, it mirrors itself to itself. But how does this inner mirroring take place? The usual answer is: consciousness is at first consciousness of the other, but, since it is consciousness throughout, whatever is present in it bathes in its light, including consciousness itself. It not only casts its light upon the things outside, it is also the source of light and transparency for itself. This explanation is correct, but it does not explain everything. It makes very clear how human consciousness essentially transcends its extraversion, it does not clarify the process whereby this transcending turns into a positive content of this consciousness. Self-consciousness, deriving from a first transcending of the intellectual knowledge of the world of objects and living things, is after all nothing more than a sense of self.

Or should we say that, by its very nature, self-consciousness can only be consciousness extended to its ultimate limit, so that it is quite useless to look for its positive content? No, on the contrary it is man's most specific essence, much more so than his consciousness is. Yet this self-consciousness always remains a consciousness; that is, the other continues to exist for it as an object. That is why it cannot exploit its "native truth" except within the sphere of this other-directedness, and provided that the other of which it is thus aware is another self-consciousness. Thus we are back at the idea from which we started, which has now been clearly verified.

CHAPTER II

From Rivalry
to Peaceful Coexistence

THE ANALYSIS OF THE STRUCTURE of self-consciousness has clearly shown that self-consciousness can reflect itself in itself only if it reflects itself in some
other self-consciousness. Man mirrors his nature in
himself to the extent that he mirrors himself in the
other person. Thus one person is for the other the living mirror in which he becomes a spectacle for himself. Not a mirror which reflects the image only in a
passive manner, but a self-seeing mirror, in which the
reflection occurs in a retro-specting glance. And all
this is reciprocal: "Its own action," says Hegel "has
also to be the action of that other."[4] Not only is the
other person the mirror of his nature for a man, but

17

he himself is likewise the mirror for the other: "Each sees the other do the same as itself; each itself does what it demands on the part of the other, and for that reason does what it does only in so far as the other does the same. Action from one side would be useless because what is to happen can only be brought about by means of both."[5] In a word, human beings can recognize each other as human beings, they can become aware of their own being human only if, by acknowledging each other's being human, each comes in himself to the awareness of his own humanness. "They recognize themselves as mutually recognizing one another."[6] This reciprocity is not an external condition of the awareness, it is an essential element of it. It belongs to the essence of becoming conscious because it belongs to the essence of man, who exists only as fellow man. "Man alone" is an ontological contradiction, hence unthinkable and impossible.

This fundamental bond-in-being does not endanger the personal subjectivity. It means only that this subjectivity always subsists, as A. Hesnard puts it, within a general intersubjectivity,[7] within "a reciprocity of existence."[8] But this unity—however essential it may be—is not a fusion, for in a fusion each selfhood would disappear in a selfless identity. Therefore the meeting of two (or more) persons is always a double (or multiple) meeting. Hegel calls this encounter *"die*

18

Mitte" (the mediating term) and adds at once that every consciousness is in itself a "*Mitte*" for the other one: "Each is the mediating term to the other, through which each mediates and unites itself with itself."[9] Should the two mediating terms coincide, we would have only a dead point and the end of every conscious relationship.

Hence, as the human relations become more real, the unity increases, but the mutual selfhood grows too; the unity will become more intimate and fruitful as the selfhood is more personal. On the other hand, the relation between persons will verge on an undifferentiated fusion if it is only a *possible* relation which has not yet developed its potentialities. No wonder, then, if we can still clearly observe the signs of this undeveloped sociality, of this "anonymous intersubjectivity,"[10] to use Hesnard's terms, in the infant during the first months of life. The small child is still living in "some kind of in-between world, he has not acquired any singular and egological perfection."[11] This is strikingly illustrated by the way in which a child sees himself in a mirror—a real mirror this time. The child believes that he is really *in the mirror,* yet at the same time he has the vague impression that he *sees* himself in the mirror.[12] The two aspects have not yet been disentangled. The child's selfhood is still too little aware of itself to keep itself altogether out of the

19

fusion. Something similar happens to the child when he begins to discover himself in the living mirror of the mother or of the environment. However, it is important to note how the child is, from the very start, beyond the dead point of a total fusion.

Out of this initial sociality, which is still mainly anonymous, the various kinds of human relations will gradually develop with increasing clearness; these relations will always contain the reciprocal acknowledgment mentioned above, while each in its own way keeps the original structure of an "identifying oneself *in* the other and *with* the other."[13]

To speak of a "gradual development of the various kinds of human relations" may sound somewhat ambiguous. One can study this development in the individual and find out what forms it gradually assumes from birth to adulthood. This is the method used by psychoanalysis. It shows how the development passes through the several stages—and the eventual conflicts —which prepare for total adaptation to social life. The legitimacy and the usefulness of such an investigation is undeniable. But there is another possible way of looking at the problem. One can study this diversity more directly within existing society, as a diversity of social life itself. In that case interest turns not so much towards the genetic development of the individual as towards these various human relations as forms of what Hegel calls *"Sittlichkeit"*—that is, the mental life of human beings insofar as it develops within society. It is especially from this point of view that we shall investigate human relations, with the intention of arriving as soon as possible at those among them which present themselves as forms of explicit human affection.

Not all forms present themselves in this way. As a matter of fact, the first forms of sociality which, dialectically considered, are the basis of the whole structure of social relations belong to an almost opposed group, that of explicit rivalry. The extreme form of this rivalry is the *"homo homini lupus*—man a wolf to man"* of Thomas Hobbes. Hobbes' error did not consist in recognizing the existence of such a situation, but in thinking that it antedated the origin of society. He did not understand that this acute opposition was a first form of unity between the opponents—or that at least it contained within itself the possibility of a positive solution. Hegel was on the right track when he claimed that out of this rivalry—which for him too becomes a life-and-death struggle—social consciousness emerges. His dialectic of the Master and the Bondsman is too well known to need comment. Moreover, commenting on it would involve us in a discussion with Hegel and slow down our investigation. This initial rivalry is, in the final analysis, nothing but the quest by men for a mutual acknowledgment of their manhood, which adopts for a time the forms of domination and subjection and fails to bring about the desired result. Ultimately it will lead to the acceptance of a necessary collaboration, based at first upon rather utilitarian motives.

This collaboration motivated by common interests may be considered as the first solid form of human relation. It will develop into a permanent element of social life, and in our present society it has grown into a huge economic structure, that of the social community of labor. Let us hasten to add that we think of every human activity which in any way performs some service for the community as having an economic aspect. It follows that the concept of labor too must be extended, that it is no longer restricted to definite forms of service. Thus even cultural services accompanied by some outside activity—as all of them are—come under the concept of labor. They too have their place in the vast economic system of exchange, of services rendered and received.

Collaboration, working together at the same task and for the common good, of itself creates only a relative unity between men. Yet one should not underestimate this unity. Its strength derives from the fact that it is absolutely necessary for the existence of the community. Were it impossible to reach a unity of collaboration, the result would be catastrophe and the downfall of man.

This collaboration in the material sphere is not yet explicit human communication. Yet it is not entirely lacking in communication of any kind. People who work together—even if only in hoisting a tree trunk— are bound to start talking to each other. Efforts must be co-ordinated, directed towards one and the same end, that end must be present in the consciousness of all, must be known and understood by everyone, etc. All this is impossible without some communication of practical insights. What this "communication" has become in the enormous system of our present world economy is self-evident.

This collaboration, made possible by continual communication, has among other results one which is important for human relations: the growing experience that human beings can come to agree, that they need each other in the pursuit of their well-being, and that this sociality as such pays high dividends.

When the work is interrupted, this experience does not evaporate. People who have worked together talk about their work. And since this talking occurs after the work has stopped, it will naturally go beyond its technical aspects. It spreads to future work, to work in general, to its conditions, its prospects, and so on. Imperceptibly the conversation begins to touch on

23

broader human interests. A turning point is reached when the talk extends to things unconnected with work, to other people, finally to personal concerns. At that point the communication clearly passes beyond the domain of practical collaboration. A sphere of mutual confidence comes into being. People begin to recognize each other as fellow men, as equals, as companions in need, who can eventually help each other. A new relationship is born, and this time a really human one. It may not be more than a relationship of comradeship. Yet here man has really found the other man.

We would be assuming too much if we took this straight off to be the awakening of human love. True, it is the first step in a direction leading eventually to explicit love, but this goal is not yet at hand. The only thing we can say is that the human relations are no longer exclusively determined by commutative interests. The mere *"do ut des*—give-and-take" mentality, although still present, has been breached. We meet with the first signs of helpfulness, a willingness to be of assistance to others not because this is useful for the group, but because the "others are human beings too." This does not bring about a great intimacy, but it does lead to an acknowledgment of the other person which goes further than in ordinary working together. This helpfulness takes many forms. The most important might be: promoting the work of the other person, helping him, acting as mediator, formal collaboration, serving in a subordinate position. We have described these forms in another book,[14] and we shall not repeat this description here.

We should not say that this helpfulness has for its inspiration and its object the other person in his uniqueness. Help is not given because the other is this unique person, with his own life and attractive qualities; the reason for the assistance given is rather, as we have said, that "he is a human being too," or, on a still lower level, because "after all, he is a human being." Furthermore, this relationship is not yet necessarily reciprocal. Unless the fact that the service is willingly rendered and readily accepted, or even received with gratitude, is to be considered as a beginning of reciprocity. Such gratitude, however, does not yet go to the other person as this person, but rather to the other person who has shown himself so human. It is to be expected that the service rendered will evoke a service in return, but this is motivated only, or at least to a great extent, by the conviction that "one service deserves another." Hence this helpfulness keeps within its essential structure some kind of ontological—even though sublimated—remainder of the commutative character of material collaboration.

Helpfulness embodies itself in the rendering of a

service. When it is considered mainly in function of this service, we may say that it is animated by an inner disposition which may be called benevolence. This is mainly a question of accent, no fine distinctions should be drawn. Benevolence is a general attitude by which one person wishes another person well, not in the sense that he merely wishes that some specific thing may happen, but in the sense that he effectively wills the good of the other, although this will does not yet lead to wholehearted activity. Benevolence is rather an attitude which brings it about that one can rely upon others when the need arises, without going so far as to expect tokens of heroic selflessness from them. It is a rather vague attitude, which pervades the whole of our life with others as a general quality, lending a tinge of social cheerfulness to the small services rendered in daily intercourse.

An accentuated form of this benevolent helpfulness is obligingness. It provides helpfulness with the power of sensing exactly—even if not into ultimate refinements—what, precisely, must be done, and how and when. It is present in the waiter who shows up at the right moment to help me with my coat and hand me my hat, in the salesgirl who wraps up my purchase in a jiffy into an elegant and handy package. Obligingness may sometimes be pushed too far and turn into obsequiousness. The proper thing then is not to mind, not even to notice, because one is aware that all things human are relative.

The rather general character of helpfulness and obligingness should not lead us to believe that the various relationships which find their specific form in the kindly rendering of services are merely the result of chance meetings. This is often the case; it is not the rule. Rendering a service generally occurs within the existing structure of organized society, in which everybody offers his services according to his profession, his function or his recognized capacity. For the services they expect people generally have to turn to certain individuals or institutions which they come upon in their environment: physicians, lawyers, judges, garage keepers, tailors, painters, officials and employees of all kinds of administrative agencies, shops, travel bureaus, theaters, restaurants, and so on. The paths over which service comes to people have been laid down to a great extent by the concrete local and social situation in which everyone lives. Helpfulness explains why all these services, requested or rendered, go beyond strict juridical or commutative relations into the domain of real human benevolence. It causes them to be rendered, above and beyond the dictates of mutual interest and just expectations, to human beings *as human beings,* with a more or less explicit intention of being at their disposal and of contributing to their human well-being.

Within these basic structures of concrete society we meet in addition the more or less haphazard and unplanned forms of obliging helpfulness. They too develop into an almost innumerable multiplicity and variety. They are more or less enduring, according to the nature of the service rendered. Thus I can get into a relation of helpfulness with somebody I meet on a cruise to Sweden or to Greece, or with somebody I encounter regularly in the same context, or with whom I sit every day in the same bus. These chance relationships may last a lifetime or amount to nothing more than a passing encounter in our everyday routine, as when, to mention only the classic examples, a stranger asks me to direct him to City Hall, or I help an old lady with a heavy suitcase or assist a man who has slipped and fallen. It is obvious that there may be great variety in the nature of the services and they may sometimes have a strong spiritual or religious content.

Thus the sphere of relations of helpfulness expands into a whole world, ultimately as wide as the world itself—the world of man which is called society. It produces a universal human trustfulness which, while having its limits and remaining somewhat relative, is nonetheless a valuable and indispensable element, the very foundation of social life. It lends to social life a certain smoothness, a matter-of-course quality, a solidity which eventually becomes capable of enduring many, and even sometimes shocking, breaches of its order. It gives social life its peaceful character, which allows it to find an orderly restfulness in itself and to run an even course that favors freedom and makes an unruffled existence possible. Life and society become agreeable, and this experience opens the way for further human relationships of a more personal nature.

· CHAPTER III ·

The Lonely Person

IT MAY SURPRISE THE READER that we now turn to the lonely person. Has the human being not broken out of his loneliness by living with others? If he has, this chapter looks like a step backwards in our study, a rather unusual procedure in dialectics. Unless, of course, the feeling of loneliness arises precisely within social life.

At any rate, loneliness is not as simple a phenomenon as the term may imply. It presents several aspects, it can be experienced on different levels. But let us first consider its relation to sociality. Not primarily because loneliness or isolation should be regarded as a failure in the expression of social tendencies. This

33

kind of loneliness does occur, and quite frequently too, and its relation to sociality is obvious. Yet one cannot, without contradiction, consider a failure of social relations as a necessary moment of these relations, since this would practically amount to admitting that they were impossible. Thus any danger of "failure" would be excluded. We are thinking of a more fundamental experience of loneliness. This will be evident when we go back to our analysis of human relationships as they have developed into peaceful coexistence.

In this peaceful coexistence men regard each other with benevolence. Their relations are no longer exclusively determined by the profit to be derived from them, their motives have been widened and modified by a real inclination to help one another. Yet this inclination remains relative. First, it has not yet entirely emerged from the economic-exchange mentality. Next, and more important, the helpfulness is still to a great extent anonymous, it is aimed at the other person as somebody who is "a human being too," as all people are. This universal helpfulness does not yet advert to the unique subjectivity of "this" individual.

Moreover, the benevolence it manifests does not generally extend beyond the service itself. Even whether it will extend to recognizing tomorrow the person treated so kindly today is not certain. Besides, there is no great desire for an acknowledgment of the

service rendered, much less for special tokens of gratitude. It looks almost as if this benevolence were as un-
aware of its own subjectivity as it is of that of the other
person. Yet this is real benevolence which wishes
others well and ministers to their well-being.

There is something ambiguous in this benevolent
helpfulness and the relations it brings about. One is
unsure of what it amounts to. It is a mixture of sym-
pathy and indifference, of attention and unconcern, of
nearness and distance, an attitude which develops for
a while only to shrink again and vanish altogether. It
surprises us as much by its sudden manifestation as by
its unexpected disappearance. Thus this helpfulness is
never quite transparent for one who experiences it, it
leaves him unsatisfied.

Is this a purely negative feeling, made up only of dissatisfaction and disappointment? Possibly, but in that
case it stops halfway and loses its deeper meaning. For
the unfinished, incomplete, halfhearted nature of this
general social benevolence opens a prospect onto further possibilities. It points towards eventual human
relations of a deeper nature. Yet as of now official helpfulness, in its own friendly way, so to speak shuts down
a glass partition between these possibilities and their
fulfillment. This gives rise to a feeling of a certain
lack. Not yet the lack of something clearly before one's
mind. For, as possibilities are only possibilities, their

eventual realization is only vaguely known: the clear consciousness of a realization is given only in and with that realization itself. It is therefore an unspecified lack, in which both what is lacking and the need itself are still experienced by way of an indistinct feeling: the feeling of a certain human dissatisfaction, a helpless sense of rejection and of being cast back onto oneself—in short, a feeling of loneliness. The individual was already lonely, now he becomes aware of this loneliness as a real situation.

Once more, however, we do not claim that this explains the whole nature of human loneliness, nor that the inhibition of human relations explained in the foregoing pages is its sole origin. What follows will show that this is by no means the case. Yet the connection established here is essential and very important. And since our purpose is to understand man in his relations with others, it is obvious that we must consider loneliness first in its social context.

One more reason for this procedure is that this will make it easier for us to avoid the danger of regarding the experience of loneliness—especially the undifferentiated feeling of loneliness—as merely a subjective state. The whole of human life is in the grip of these experiences, they are not phenomena occurring only within a subject closed to the world and to others. Such a subject is an unreal abstraction. Life in the

36

world and in the group is essential for man. He has a
natural orientation towards others; he is other-directed
even in his loneliness. He can feel lonely and isolated
only in his living together with things and people.
Therefore his loneliness is something which will cast a
pall upon this whole network of relations. What is
more: not only is it true that man can feel lonely only
within the group, his loneliness itself is already a form
of sociality. In other words, man not only experiences
his loneliness *as* a social being, he can feel lonely only
because he is by nature social. It is within this context
that the whole dialectics of loneliness works itself out.

The presence of such dialectics makes it clear that
man's loneliness is not an even and undivided moment of his emotional life. It is from the very start a
restless experience of division within himself, a dis-
sociation. It is compounded of eager desire and painful
lack, eventual possibility without substance in the
present. As a consciousness of future possibilities it
continually projects the fulfillment of its desires. But
for the time being it is an imaginary fulfillment, whose
repercussions emphasize the fact that one is alone. This
first experience is negative, even explicitly negative;
without being a frustration or a failure of attempts
made for more human contacts, it is nevertheless nothing but a deepening of one's loneliness. And since we
should not overlook its connection with the world of

people and things, it is also the experience of the barren presence of the great wide world, which encircles the lonely person with its cold aloofness.

This is a dangerous moment for the lonely person, beyond which many feel unable to advance. It is dangerous because his natural confidence in his own possibilities can become so weakened as practically to dissolve, leaving him with only a sterile yearning to settle down in his loneliness. This danger can be avoided by keeping one's attention on the other person in spite of everything and continuing to show him benevolence. Looking away from oneself and refusing to withdraw for good into solitude is the only way of making the momentous discovery for which one is now ready, the discovery of the loneliness of all human beings.

It may seem that we are using a big word for this new experience when we call it a "discovery." Yet it is a discovery—this sudden noticing of what one had not yet seen, or at least not yet fully realized. "I have known for a long time that everyone is lonely," says Nina, the heroine of Luise Rinser's novel *Mitte des Lebens.*[15] In other words: It is a long time since I made this discovery, but there was a time when I had not made it. That time is required for this discovery may be explained by two reasons. First, the lonely person is by nature too occupied with himself, even though his basic orientation is towards others. In this other-directedness he nevertheless remains steeped in his own "ego." This makes him watch without perception what goes on in the "ego" of others. Especially—and this is the second reason—since the others with whom life brings him into contact meet him so peacefully and so helpfully. In this helpfulness, which is not directed to the "I" of the person, the "I" of the others, too, remains hidden. The general atmosphere which this helpfulness lends to collective life—in a business, in a large city, etc.—does not convey the impression that people are dissatisfied or unhappy. On the contrary, everything is pervaded with an official, well-meaning orderliness, availability and friendliness, with all their nuances ranging from the male's equable readiness to be of service to the female's smiling obligingness. This smiling friendliness especially has its stereotyped forms: the salesgirl smile, the secretary smile, the hostess smile, the television smile, the star smile, the camera smile, the "folksy" smile, the cheesecake smile, the advertisement smile, etc. One has, as it were, to catch people outside the official role they play in society before one gets an inkling of the fact that often their cheerful, busy kindliness masks a great loneliness. At once the experience of one's own loneliness assumes quite a different aspect. Now a man sees his loneliness in the loneliness of others, no longer feeling it as something which sets him apart. He senses himself at one with the "mass of the lonely ones." The experience of loneliness has become the experience of the loneliness of all human beings, and this universality suddenly becomes a possible bond. Since the others too are lonely, the person is no longer alone in being lonely. Loneliness itself is discovered as a potential companionship, especially since the revelation of it in others suddenly endows it with a positive aspect. For the experience of loneliness testifies to the presence of a deeper human self-identity, of a hidden but real intimacy with an inalienable self.

Moreover, this discovery is not the experience of an isolated individual, it is always a mutual experience between persons. This reciprocity is already in itself human contact, it is a real encounter, empty at first, but one which will turn spontaneously into a search for further reciprocity. Thus the feeling of loneliness —provided it refuses to shut itself in—becomes finally a moment, perhaps a necessary moment, of the growth of sociality. It will give social relations a steadiness which they would never have without it.

Does this mean that loneliness is the only incentive bringing people together? Certainly not. And this will be easily understood when we recall that man would not feel lonely if he were not social. Loneliness must not make us leave the social drive out of account. It is because of this drive that the lonely person will refuse to shut himself up in himself. But we must also consider the other side of the picture: it is equally true that the other person—who is not designed to merge with a herd of his kind—cannot experience his sociality without becoming aware of his inalienable intimacy with himself and his unique individuality. It is therefore from both these experiences that men reach out for each other. The social tendency is positive, spontaneous, matter-of-course. The experience of loneliness is wavering, awkward and uncertain in its social aspects. It endows the social tendency with a discretion, a thoughtfulness, a tact, a considerateness and even a delicacy, which will grace the encounter with the other with an eminently personal character. For it has an exceptional feeling for the singular, the unique, in which it has undergone the experience of itself.

The rise of concrete relations on this level of real human reciprocity is an achievement; that is, it is not a mere chance, for chance, which is nothing but blind coincidence, can never explain a unity of human beings as human, since these human beings themselves are involved in it with their free personalities. It becomes a progressive strategy of exploration—approaching, gradually weighing each other's qualities and discovering more and more possibilities—culminating in the gladdening evidence that they can get along with one another; finally a real finding of each other in mutual affection.

This "finding" does not, however, erase the experience of loneliness. For no characteristic of spirit is ever lost. Nor has initial rivalry disappeared. Both characteristics belong permanently to the structure of all human relations, however completely these relations may transcend them. We must therefore expect to find them again later on, although under other forms. Meanwhile we may be beginning to wonder whether man will ever be totally cured of his loneliness.

· CHAPTER IV ·

Human Affection

THE STILL VERY IMPERSONAL benevolence which pervaded what we have called peaceful coexistence develops, in the new situation which arises now, into a real affection, by which human beings unite in the authentic core of their being. The variety of relations among men made possible by life in the world and in society explains why the bonds of affection which grow in these relations are also of various kinds and will surely not have the same manifestations. We shall presently consider their main forms. But first it will be useful to examine a general structure which these forms, *mutatis mutandis,* have in common. Of its very nature such an examination will remain unfinished.

On the other hand, it would be inadvisable to treat directly of the main forms of affection themselves, although they are more concrete, for this would entail the danger of overlooking the deeper reality they bring to light and ignoring the totality within which they have their complementary function.

The transition from impersonal benevolence to affection is accompanied by a twofold phenomenon. First, we note that in the coupling of benevolence and service rendered this benevolence gradually gains the ascendancy. The service becomes, as it were, subordinate, even while remaining very real. What one feels matters more than what one does for the other. Moreover, the feeling loses more and more of its vague generality. It is directed now towards the other person, who is no longer an undetermined "somebody" but is treated as a real "thou." The service itself, as we shall see later, acquires another meaning.

Obligingness was still an indirect relation. The contact it created became concrete in the service. The two persons who came into touch with each other were both concentrating on the service, the service rendered and received. They talked to each other, they knew that they had dealings with each other, but they were not yet looking at each other. Their eyes hardly met because the service interposed itself between them. It brought them together, but it also kept them apart.

When benevolence really emerges they look up, they take their eyes off the service, they see each other. The wavering line of their glance straightens out into the freedom of a direct mutual beholding.

Thus affection is born in an atmosphere which is quite different from that of the previous relationships. It is an atmosphere of expansion, of openness in relation to the other person, and for *this* other person in his existential identity. This identity is a revelation and an amazing discovery, but not one that occurs as if by magic. We might perhaps call it more precisely a voyage of discovery, an ever renewed expedition into unknown territory, with new vistas constantly opening up on the horizon.

Affection gets off to a timid start. Various vague ways of behaving manifest a desire of giving up the rigid seclusion of one's own "difference." The person turns towards the other, he looks at him, he shows himself to him in the very glance by which he observes and considers the other. He steps outside himself—or, at least, he starts to move in that direction—outside his encapsuled loneliness, his human singularity, his hidden, unfathomable inacessibility; outside the fortress of his individuality. He makes himself available, even though his attempt may be full of hesitation. But even such an attempt would not be made were it not elicited by some corresponding movement in the other,

47

or at least by the fact that he suspects in the other a certain inclination to a similar attempt. From the very start there is an interaction based upon a consonance which remains mostly unconscious.

Two human beings have stepped outside themselves. As Hegel puts it, they have proceeded into *"die Mitte"* (the mediating term), where they have met each other. It looks as if some point between them were now occupied by their mutual presence. But such an impression can be misleading. We should be in danger of fixating the encounter in a wrong image, which might confuse all our further reflections. For, strictly speaking, there is no such thing as a point of meeting between the two persons which, having hitherto constituted a division between them, would now serve as their rendezvous. For they withheld themselves from each other, and what thus kept them apart can be removed only *in themselves*. Human beings do not make contact with each other like physical forces or chemical elements whose fusion produces a third something. The encounter takes place simply *in the self-consciousness of each of them*. It is therefore a *double encounter*. One person meets the other in the self-consciousness of the other person: *Jedes (Selbst-bewusstsein) ist dem andern die Mitte*—Each (self-consciousness) is the mediating term to the other one. "Moreover, this double encounter itself is a twofold encounter, since each, while meeting the other, also meets itself. For "each is the mediating term to the other, through which each mediates and unites itself with itself; and each is to itself and to the other an immediate self-existing reality."[16] In affection, finding the other is inseparably connected with finding oneself, and the other way round. Seeing the other—which, in affection, becomes seeing and liking—sheds more light upon one's own nature. Each enters the limelight cast by another consciousness, and in so doing, each comes within the luminous sphere of his own radiation which, while illuminating the other, is reflected in his own consciousness.

Thus we note that affection at the very outset contains a complex structure. It is by no means a sentimental fusion of persons. Structure implies opposition. This opposition was formerly an open rivalry. Although by now it has been overcome, it persists somehow as overcome. While it may be transcended by an increasing intimacy, it nevertheless continues to make itself felt as that which is transcended. The same is true for loneliness, which is equally part of the essential structure. This loneliness will increasingly be experienced as a loneliness in common. Affection is born, not because people are really drawn out of their loneliness, but because their loneliness has become an open loneliness. They are no longer lonely "alone," no longer lonely only for themselves, they are lonely for each other. This being for each other is a real unity, a real communion and a sharing in each other. But what is thus shared is at first only their mutual loneliness.

It is worthwhile to linger a few moments on this essential structure. We have shown that it implies an internal opposition, which is gradually overcome by unification, without ever being eliminated by total unity. We must consider it as a permanent potential moment whose continued presence within the total structure explains why human love will never lack a certain imperfection. But this imperfection is not a set limit beyond which affection cannot proceed. We should rather consider it as an incapacity for affection to reach its term. Affection, like the human being himself, will always remain limited. Such limitation belongs to its nature, even as it belongs to the nature of man. Therefore this opposition is not only a limiting but a constitutive element. This means that affection, however intense, will always include some exteriority between the loving subject and the one loved. It follows that not only will the granting of affection always be conditioned by the receptivity of the loved subject, but further, the loving subject will always try, to some extent, to appropriate the beloved as his own possession. This inevitably introduces a kind of duality into their affection, and almost a double intentionality. This too belongs to its nature and is a manifestation of its essential imperfection. Every token of affection involves some appropriation of the person to whom affection is shown. In this sense every *love of benevolence* is wrapped in a *love of concupiscence,* because the very granting of affection remains the *possession* of the one who grants it. Man is unable to give himself unreservedly. Even when the utmost unselfishness is achieved, the selflessness of love will return as his *own* perfection to the one who practices it. This means a defect, not in the perfection itself, but in the fact that it can never be experienced in such a way that it becomes identically the perfection of the one loved. It is not necessary to strive towards such an ideal, for its realization can only be deceptive; an inhuman fusion of two beings is confused with absolute love.

The constitutive limitation of affection does not alter the fact that people who like each other have really discovered each other in the uniqueness of their personality. But this "having discovered" each other does not mean the instantaneous perfection of their relationship. Here again we meet the same limit and potentiality. The mutual discovery means only that a previous "not discovering" has come to an end, it does not mean that the discovery is at once total and exhaustive. This discovery is an outcome, but one which changes at once into a new beginning. What has been discovered is ultimately a new possibility. This discovery is more amazing in the perspectives it reveals than in its substantial content. A new country has been discovered but not yet explored. The journey has just begun.

The unknown invites us to explore it. But we should not forget that this unknown is the unknown identity of a free personality, of a human being who is a self. This is not an impersonal attraction but an invitation, the offer of human hospitality, a freely extended welcome to step inside. Furthermore, since everything here turns on reciprocity and since this reciprocity is in some sense the element out of which everything grows, a one-sided invitation is not enough. It would amount to opening the door to an unknown stranger, who might soon turn out to be a troublesome guest or a dangerous intruder.

Nor should we conceive of this exploration as a matter of gaining access to a purely spiritual space, advancing together into an immaterial intimacy incapable of expression in words, one whose mysterious invisibility puts it beyond the reach of our senses. Undoubtedly real affection aims at the spiritual selfhood of man. But this selfhood is not encountered in an abstract interiority uprooted from concrete existence. Human beings do not feel affection for each other outside the context of life, outside the world in which life is lived. They embrace each other in their whole human reality. In affection, as in self-consciousness, "the whole expanse of the world of sense is conserved,"[17] although everything acquires a new meaning. Whereas living in loneliness—at least at its worst moments—made the world appear meaningless, now everything acquires a meaning. No longer only the utilitarian meaning of economics, or the peaceful meaning of universal friendly living together, but a personal, human meaning. Living together in affection changes the face of the world, which is now transformed into the concrete situation of affection itself. The world is seen with the same deeply human look which people who like each other exchange. The world too becomes an object of affection. This way of looking at the objects in the world transforms them into almost human realities. They reflect the disposition of which they have become the concrete situation. For the world is always what man makes of it. That is why affection makes the world exist in a wholly different way, a hitherto dormant value awakens in all things. This value does not consist merely in the subjective and external symbolization of an experience occurring first in an acosmic interiority before being manifested externally. On the contrary, the world is a constitutive element of the concrete reality of this experience itself. Affection finds in the endless diversity of the world's phenomena a symphonic rendition of her one and undivided theme. And again, this is not because affection projects on them a meaning superimposed from without, but because it creates a meaning which raises the very essence of reality. Thus the exercise of affection itself becomes an authentic cosmic event. It renders the world good for men; and, at the same time, the mediation of the world makes of affection a concrete reality.

In this new world affection sees the whole of nature with new and eager eyes, and nature in turn lends to affection some of her own unspoiled charm. The world of culture too feels affection's magic touch and is raised to a higher level of humanity. Affection permeates the home with its many familiar objects, the cultural environment of city or of dwelling place; affection thrives in a common interest for literature, music, science, historical events, and so on. There is even more. The world of man himself, the whole of social life, comes under the influence of affection. Even though most of the relations which bind us to others remain on the level of general benevolence, this benevolence, without losing its relative and limited character, is shown in a wholly different spirit. The negative features we have described lose their negative repercussion upon our mood because the lack of human warmth felt in this benevolence has been removed by affection. It is obvious how all this promotes benevolence itself.

This transformed world is, of course, no parallel vision of single individuals. It is a reality and a spectacle which is seen by one and the same glance. Affection unifies not only the persons but also their feelings, their thoughts and their insights. Yet that unity of vision is not a fusion of consciousness, since here again a sublimated rivalry keeps its rights as a necessary constitutive element. This rivalry develops into an enriching interaction and a mutual mediation. It becomes the inner ferment of a complementary deepening. Each of the partners in affection sees the world not only in union with the other but also with the eyes of the other. Their vision is a shared vision. They see each other in seeing the world, and they see the world in the look they direct upon each other. The double *Mitte* to which we have referred remains unchanged. Hence the two not only find each other in mutual comprehension and good will, but they also bestow on each other a vision and comprehension of the whole world. This communication is not something which happens once and for all; it is a ceaseless interaction between the affection itself, as it undergoes growth and transformation, and the world—subject of its very nature to constant, restless change—as it exercises its animating mediation. Thus affection as it looks into the world is a real *life,* which, like all life, renews itself unceasingly.

It is remarkable that, unlike the forms of human relations we considered earlier, affection has from the beginning a decidedly contemplative character. This is not surprising, since every relation and every activity, as it becomes more true and more real, is more clearly aware of its essential content—its "truth," as Hegel puts it—and grasps it more intuitively. But we should be going too far if we saw in affection nothing but an act of contemplation. The concrete awareness of the mutual unification is also, to the same extent, something which happens. The content does not exist without the realization. As something taking place in the world this realization assumes the form of work. And although it would be erroneous to separate this active aspect from the more intuitive aspect, and inexpedient even to distinguish it too much, it would not help us to grasp the meaning of affection if we lumped all these aspects together in utter confusion.

This shared contemplative appropriation of the world becomes a shared active emergence into the world, a shared performance of a task, of some work. According to the nature and the stability of the bonds of affection, this work may become a life's work. It is mainly in activity that affection experiences its reality, even as it became aware of itself ideally in contemplation. This experience of its reality is a direct experience, because in collaboration affection itself is at work; as the soul of this collaboration, it becomes active, it manifests its fecundity, it realizes itself as affection. But it is also a mediated experience, insofar as it comes about in and through the work which takes shape. In the work it experiences itself objectively as a creative power, so that the collaboration turns into an undivided power and embodies itself in a unique objectivity.

Yet this unique and undivided objectivity of the thing done or the task accomplished is not a homogeneous unity—and it is no quirk on the author's part which makes him continually remind the reader of this complementary aspect, but reality itself. The character of reciprocity, essential in every human relation, will not wholly disappear in this objectivity. First because the work is the result of a continual collaboration of persons, who are capable of this collaboration only on account of their complementary, hence of their somewhat opposed, identities. Next because the work, as undivided result of this collaboration, retains a double meaning. For not only has this work been done by two (or more) persons together, but these persons have undertaken it for each other. In that sense the work of affection is still a "service." It differs from the eco-

nomically utilitarian service in that the service of affection is not bartered for some other service. The bartering—which *ipso facto* reaches a higher degree of
sublimation—takes place, as it were, in one and the
same service. It consists in this: that the persons collaborating show and practice their affection by aiming
the work accomplished together at each other. The
perfection of this mutual giving and receiving consists
in the unicity of that which is given and received. Because of this perfection the service rises above its mere
utilitarian value and—without becoming useless—
turns into a direct token of the mutual affection and
its very reality. Should this double meaning disappear, the work would lose most of its meaning. It
would simply be something which happens to be done,
it would dwindle into a mere matter of business.

Although the fact of collaborating for one another
coincides with affection, the product of this collaboration always keeps a certain exteriority with respect to
the feelings which inspire it. This exteriority is even
more evident in a phenomenon which is very typical of
affection, the gift. Giving something is a certain "doing," just as working is. But while the work is brought
about by working, the gift already exists before it is
given. Giving implies forsaking something one has on
behalf of somebody else. It is obvious that sooner or
later the gift may be repaid with some gift in return,

but this does not belong so immediately to the essence of the gift. The same is true of the expectation that such a return gift may be forthcoming. The gift as such stands totally outside the economic sphere, in which everything consists in the bartering of equivalent services. This trans-economical character of the gift does not exclude the possibility of its having some economic usefulness. Yet this usefulness is not an essential quality of the gift, unless one extends the notion of the economically useful so far as to include an element of contemplation. There is no major objection to such an extension, but it would force us to revise many current opinions. Of course, it is possible to do something in some way or other with everything: one can wear a diamond, enjoy looking at a painting, brighten one's room with a bouquet. Yet the real meaning of the gift does not consist mainly in what one can do with it or in the mere transfer of ownership. We have not far to look for its real meaning: the gift means the affection itself with which it is bestowed. It *is* this affection embodied in a gesture.

But of itself the gift does not guarantee absolute faithfulness. It aims at such faithfulness, but it can do this only within the situation of the present moment. It is meant to be binding on the whole future, but it cannot control this future. Nobody is certain of what is to come, nor of his own future affection. But this uncertainty (we might call it a metaphysical uncertainty) does not affect the gift, it is even positively excluded. A true gift explicitly implies such an exclusion. It is given *for good,* along with the affection with which it is offered.

We have already remarked that the gift does not involve the expectation of a gift in return, even though the latter will eventually be forthcoming. Nevertheless one who receives a gift is put in an awkward position. If he repays what he receives at once with a return gift, it will look as if he were not allowing himself the time for—nor the donor the pleasure of—a delighted contemplation of the gift. The first requirement of authentic affection is *not* to wonder what I can give in return, but to linger a while in rejoicing because of the token of affection which—unexpectedly, albeit not quite unexpectedly—I have thus received. Repaying too quickly may produce the impression that I wish to reverse the gift, to settle my account at once. This would lead us back into an economic barter relationship. Does this mean that I should not show my gratitude for the gift? Of course not. I must be grateful, but not too explicitly, because an effusive gratitude, too, may turn into something which looks almost like an anxiety to get even with the gift. The basic attitude remains one of sincere surprise and of joy because of the increase in affection to which the gift testifies. Pondering how I, in my turn, may surprise the other becomes more authentic when I take my time doing it.

The very nature of affection shows that this answer to the gift is the authentic answer. For affection consists in liking one another, liking to be and to live with one another, mutually enjoying one another's company, being happy together. But the gift is nothing but the concrete token of these feelings. Therefore the answer to it will consist mainly in a rejoicing because of the gift, being happy on account of it, and sincerely manifesting this joy and happiness.

Moreover, such a reaction to the gift takes away the apparent one-sidedness of the gift, which—however one may look at it—would not quite harmonize with the basic trend characterizing this whole sphere of human relationships. Real reciprocity can only be a polarity of *liking* to give and *liking* to receive, for this polarity permeates the identical joy and the identical happiness so specific for affection.

CHAPTER V

Affection and Love

THERE IS NO COMPELLING REASON for putting an end to our analysis of affection. Besides, that is not what we are doing when we speak of human love, for it is difficult to claim that there is a difference between the two which amounts to an essential distinction. What puts love above affection is rather the intense, definitive and utterly personal manner in which it is exercised. We do not say that this does not involve any formal difference. On the contrary, true love actualizes moments which remain more or less implicit in ordinary affection. As to finding out where precisely the boundary between the two of them lies, that is a question of slight philosophical importance, since it contributes nothing to our insight into the phenomenon itself.

One way of discovering how we pass, or rather how we ascend, from affection to love is to continue our analysis of the phenomenon of the gift. We have said that the gift, as a token of affection, would lose its whole meaning if one saw in it only the transfer of a useful possession. It nevertheless is a possession, the object of some act of having and, as such, to some extent external to *being* affectionate. But *having* and *being* are not without connection. Suppose we interpret being in some way as *being oneself*—wherein "being" is used as a transitive verb whose content is "oneself"—and affection, therefore, as *being oneself for others*—whereby whatever is included in *being oneself* passes into the *being oneself of the other person*—then *having* is primarily the outward manifestation of all this. It manifests the *being outside itself* of this *being oneself*. This *being outside itself* is essential for the being of man. The first content of this *having* is nothing but the outward appearance of the person himself, his being-in-the-world. This *having-being* is therefore not closed to the world; it rather comprises this world within itself. In short, the basic and essential *having* of man is the personal way in which he does his existing in the world and in which this world —although it belongs at once to all human beings—is *his world*. Possessing something by way of individual ownership is only the most material form and the outer limit of this kind of *having*.

Hence we may not simply add being and having together as two merely opposed realities. On the other hand, we are not allowed to put them on the same level, as equivalent and complementary aspects of reality. For being finds its meaning in itself, not in its being outside itself, whereas the latter discovers its meaning and explanation only in being. In short, although having is to some extent complementary to being, it is forever transcended by it. Being is the meaning of having and not the other way round. Being does not simply lend meaning to having, not because the world of having would in its turn transcend the realm of being—as is held by those who confuse transcendence with endlessness—but because that world remains forever excluded from the domain of the spirit.

The same relationship exists in a gift. Hence that which is properly offered in a gift—despite what has been said of its exteriority—cannot be simply something external, some object of mere having. It is rather, in its concrete shape and availability, the reality itself of the affection which people feel for each other. Hence the gift is the visible form of an active relationship, and it will be a real gift to the extent in which it is offered as identified with this attitude. Therefore the more meaning the thing given has for the donor, the more it belongs to his intimate self and contains something of himself, the more he himself, with all his affection, will be represented in his gift. This identity reaches its perfection when the person no longer only *gives* what he *has,* but is able to give what he *is.* Then the gift coincides with the act of giving itself, and the affection assumes the form of a donation of oneself. It is this affection in its fullness which we call love.

Does this mean that love is raised above all externalities and thrives in a purely spiritual realm? Obviously not. Even in love, however spiritual it is, man will not deny his nature. What raises love above affection is not that it is divorced from its living context. What is new in love is that in it human affection reaches a point of completeness hitherto unknown—even though all affection by nature aims at such completeness.

Does love mean the terminal point of all human relations? Do they reach their ultimate perfection in this transcendence of affection, or, if one prefers it, in this fulfillment of affection in love? We must deny this. For, once more, the stage we have reached manifests its potentiality. It contains all its wealth only as a possibility. Only the evidence of this possibility has become manifest. A new life has opened out, but it is not yet fulfilled.

It is typical of man that this fulfillment can take place only through the unrestricted mediation of concrete life. And thus once more we meet in love the whole structure of affection, although on a much deeper level.

The discovery of the other person with which affection started was a revelation; the discovery of the other person in love is an even more amazing revelation. Affection too discovered the other person in his identity, and it is precisely this which puts it above mere benevolence. But this identity of the other was seen as *equivalent* to one's own, and the awareness of this equivalence was the specific reason for the joy born of affection. But in love this equivalence is broken; hence the overwhelming effect of true love. For love really believes in the absolute value of the beloved, who in love is always held to be greater and incomparably more valuable than the loving subject, because real love of its essence aims at the absolute. The absolute is its only object, all other objects leave it unsatisfied. However much the lover may grow in love, he always feels small, poor, powerless, the lesser of the two. Every donation of himself is felt as imperfect in contrast to the loveliness of the beloved. Not only with reference to God, but also with reference to another human being, authentic love is the flower of humility. It is as essential for love to overlook the human limitation of the beloved as to become aware of its own insufficiency; thus it welcomes love received in return like some unlooked for happiness.

But this is a reciprocal relationship. The experience of one is also that of the other. This restores equality in fact. But neither partner is conscious of this restoration, neither pays any attention to it. They see only the absolute value of the person they love, who is for both their all in all at which their love is aimed. The whole relationship turns into a vital awareness of their mutual transcendence—or, better, of their being transcended. The giving of oneself is lost, as it were, in the joy of being accepted. And since this being accepted occurs in the fullest personal freedom, it contains in its turn the self-donation of the other, his whole essential and basic orientation towards the one whose love he receives. Because of the transcendent value each attaches to the donation that is received, both partners feel that it is incomparably more precious than the donation to which it is a response. Thus both escape the limitation of their own selves; the contemplation of the loveliness of the other delivers each from the constriction of the individual self.

This at least is the fundamental disposition wherein the relation of person to person is transformed into love. But the presence of this disposition does not yet imply its complete development. Although the disposition of love can come into being very suddenly with unshakable evidence of mutual desire for each other, even then it is only an ideal; it can be transformed into reality only through the mediation of concrete life, with all its work and woe, its elements of surprise and unexpectedness, its joys and its pains, its successes and its disappointments. That is why human love consists much more in the unconditional will of *becoming* everything for each other than in the present ability of *being* everything for each other. In this whole process love is the will to make the other person exist in his identity and *in himself* only because he is worthy of my love, and of accomplishing this by living wholly for him. Only the effective expression of love can reveal what this means.

In this revelation the insight will slowly develop— and this is the ultimate test of love's authenticity— that "making the other exist" extends to much more than his simple "being there," his mere physical life, what Hegel calls *"das natürliche Bestehen"* (the natural existence) or *"die natürliche Position"* (the natural position).[18] This natural position has already been transcended in the emergence of self-consciousness. It is only by putting himself above life that man can reach an insight into himself in mutual recognition between himself and another. Yet this self-consciousness will soon realize that it can detach itself only from a life that is quite real, hence that this life is as indispensable to self-consciousness as is this self-consciousness itself. Whatever one may think of Hegel's assertion, whether or not it implies a real transcending of life and death, love sooner or later faces the problem of a transcending of life—in other words, love faces the uncertainty of physical life with which it is bound up, it faces the threat of death.

According to the nature of love this threat, again, becomes a double experience *and* a unique experience. As a unique experience this threat foresees the death of love itself; as a double experience it foresees the loss of the beloved, the loss of his presence or of the possibility of loving him any longer. But because of its absolute character love cannot acquiesce in this prospect. Of its very nature it desires permanence, and above all—owing to its transcendent orientation towards the other person—it demands the continuance in being of the loved one. Real love does not wane under this threat. Hence it is as strong as death. Is it even stronger than death? At any rate, such is its basic desire and even its most fundamental will. It wants to love and to exist forever, to love and to exist beyond life and death. Of its very nature it intimates immortality, and it carries this immortality in its consciousness.

CHAPTER VI

Love and Transcendence

OUR ANALYSIS OF AFFECTION and love has been placing increasing emphasis on the identity of the person. Yet we have not said much about that identity in itself. Is it possible to say much about it? Is it not the inaccessible secret of every human being? It has been defined as the "incommunicability of the person." If this definition is correct, there seems to be no way of access to it. And worse still, our conception of love as utterly personal communication threatens to collapse.

The definition of the human person as "an individual substance endowed with a rational nature" is of little help here. This may be perfectly serviceable when it is used as a definition; as a characterization of the inner person it does not take us very far. Hence we prefer to view personality—without in the least questioning its rational, individual or substantial character—as the absolute value of spiritual selfhood. Of course the term "absolute" must be explained, for absolute means wholly unconditioned. Can we claim that man is thus wholly unconditioned? Is he not rather what we call a "contingent" being, a being that exists but might well not exist? an essentially relative being?

Unquestionably, yes. But what is the meaning of this relativity? A thing is relative when it does not have the ground of its existence in itself. This is true for the human being. He is really himself, but he is not himself the cause of his being. Therefore he must, according to the traditional demonstration, find the cause of his existence in another being. Should the latter, too, be relative, the problem is not solved but pushed a step further back. Ultimately man must find the reason for his existence in a being which is not relative, in an absolute Being, in God. Moreover, we are speaking here of the relativity of a real *self*, of a being *which is itself*. Such a being is aware of itself, it knows itself for what it is, it is explicitly conscious of its relativity as relativity. Or, in other words, it sees its relativity as not-absolute; hence it experiences it as a *relation to the absolute*.

In this way human relativity reveals its true nature.

For here relative means that "which stands in relation," it points towards a positive ontological connection, towards a "being one with." In man's relativity a relation of unity with God is implicit. And this sheds a totally new light on his situation. The relativity which reduces man to a limited being is also that by means of which he transcends this limit. It becomes for him a means of access to the absolute Being, an absolute Being which is one with man's being—because it is the cause of this being—and which, nevertheless, transcends it infinitely.

We use the word "transcend" because it is the classical term for what we mean. Yet this term may evoke a visual image which does not quite fit the meaning, the image of rising above something extrinsically. The "transcendent" may then be visualized as something which rises so much above the thing transcended that it leaves it, as it were, far below itself. This, of course, is not the real meaning of transcendence, but the image in which the mind tries to grasp this real meaning may inadvertently have so much effect that the false connotation is inescapable. The choice of this image is perhaps to be explained by the fact that the mentality which produces it is primarily turned towards the objective world. As soon as we shift the emphasis towards the more subjective aspects of being, we are led, in the nature of the case, to consider the

77

fact of "being transcended" as a *depth,* a depth which reveals unfathomable abysses of being, which hints at some mysterious interiority never to be plumbed by any consciousness, a divine creative presence more interior to man than his most intimate selfhood—*"interior intimo meo,"* in the words of Augustine.

However we may try to put into human words this mysterious relationship, one thing is certain: man has precisely in this relationship, hence in his relativity, a truly absolute value, which consists in his ontological oneness with God. This oneness is not added to his nature, it is not a mere property. It *is* his very nature. For without this oneness man is absolutely nothing. However, this oneness is necessarily limited. For a total oneness with God would suppress contingency altogether and make every contingent being utterly impossible. Hence, although man is one with the divine ground of his being, and although this oneness with God constitutes his nature, man is also *other than God.* This *being other* which separates man from God makes of the oneness a relation without taking away the absolute value of this relation; despite the restricting otherness, it remains a relation of oneness with the absolute Being.

Important consequences derive from all this, not only for the nature of the person but also for the nature of human love. The nature of the person is wholly misunderstood if one conceives it as a "being locked up in oneself." On the contrary, it is essentially an "*esse ad*," a "being towards," an "openness" to, the absolute Being. This "being towards God" constitutes the deepest ground of man's selfhood, and it explains the incommunicability of selfhood. It is beyond all communication because it comprises a transcendence which makes its ontological content unfathomable and as such incommunicable. Therefore the incommunicability is not so much the result of some kind of subjective inaccessibility, but rather of a superabundance of *being*. The impossibility of expressing oneself comes from the overwhelming fullness of that which is to be expressed.

Yet incommunicability is not merely positive, it also includes a negative moment. The relativity which makes man into an ontological relation to God involves the fact that he is limited in his being. But every limitation, from whatever angle one looks at it, is rooted in non-being. Man is and is not. Being and not-being are equally constitutive of his nature. Selfhood has a negative side. Being oneself comprises an element of being other. This not only inserts it into some cosmic *being outside oneself,* it makes it also *other* than *every other* human selfhood, it drives it into utter individuality. This individuality, too, is incommunicable, but for a quite different reason. It is incom-

79

municable—or, as some prefer to say, ineffable—simply because it contains hardly anything which can be said of it or communicated about it; in short, because it borders upon nothingness. And all the so-called individuating notes by which one tries to grasp this individuality are—as Hegel has shown[19]—nothing but generalities which apply to an indefinite number of individuals.

Therefore incommunicability is a very ambivalent notion. And we are not helped by speaking of an *incommunicability of the person* and an *ineffability of the individual,* since incommunicability and ineffability are perfectly convertible. Ineffability is nothing but the intuitive aspect of incommunicability, while the latter refers more to the active aspect. Hence we should not look for a difference of positivity and negativity between "incommunicable" and "ineffable." Such a difference does exist between personality and individuality. As personality man is spiritual selfhood, inner self-identity; as individuality he is exteriority to himself, a being outside himself in the element of otherness. Therefore individuality is a limitation of the person, although this limitation belongs to his nature. It explains why man exists as a plurality, as always other, as limited. Nevertheless this distinction between personality and individuality is only relative. However opposed to each other, they do not exist outside each other. Their only reality is the unity of the *individual person*.

The same is true for what we may call positive and negative incommunicability. Both exist only as moments of one and the same incommunicability. This brings us nearer to a solution of the antinomy, that human love ought to be some kind of communication of that which is incommunicable. The meeting of positive and negative incommunicability is a meeting of man's *transcendence* with his unceasing *otherness*. Through the meeting of these two elements, transcendence enters the world of concrete experience and otherness escapes its mere negativity. It becomes a concrete manifestation of the transcendent relation to the absolute Being, hence also of the spiritual selfhood. When we say that the negative incommunicability of individuality escapes its mere negativity, we mean that it acquires a positive meaning, not that it would lose its incommunicability and its ineffability. On the contrary, it is as ineffability, but this time as a phenomenally visible ineffability, that it makes manifest the transcendent incommunicability of the spirit.

Does this imply that the transcendence of the person has found an adequate expression in its individual and ineffable way of appearing? By no means. This would at once rob it of its transcendent and absolute character. Only this has happened: the absolute mys-

tery of the spiritual personality, its hidden and unfathomable unity with itself and with God, has now
really entered into the phenomenal world. In this
world it really manifests itself, but it manifests itself as
it is, hence as fundamentally incommunicable. What
we see is the mystery of the person, and we see it only
as a mystery.

The mysterious depth which reveals itself in every
human being is not some kind of universal value
which is encompassed only in a superficial way by the
singularity of this person. It exists only *by way of its
irreplaceable individuality.* Through its union with the
individual otherness it turns into an ever new and surprising reality. It passes beyond all dualism and iden-
tifies itself with the most singular identity of the
person. On account of this ever renewed and new existence in every human being, it gives to the person an
immense *originality.* Something is original when it
bears its origin in itself, when it is identified with that
origin and shows this identity in its exterior manifestations. Every human being is original because he himself is, in his singular reality, a relation to his Origin,
because he himself originates in inalienable identity
from the Source of all being. Every human being is
placed in existence immediately by God's infinite Selfhood as a unique self-being spirit. That is why in his

identity he reveals an ever renewed manifestation of a divine *likeness*.

That in which this likeness becomes transparent is the personal individuality. But this supposes that we do not restrict this individuality to a determination deriving from "dimensive quantity." Carefully considered, that determination contains many more besides quantitative dimensions. When we consider individuality only as a connection with dimensive quantity, we reduce it to an extreme limitation or potentiality. On the other hand, concrete individuality is the complete unfolding of this extreme potentiality into the whole historicity of a singular human existence. It is man's life insofar as it takes shape as a cosmic event, insofar as it unfolds as a visible spectacle in human society. Man's individuality is the history of his whole life, the totality of his actions, works and conduct as it influences the world of things and of men and gives shape to his spiritual identity as a cosmic event. Yet this individual cosmic manifestation of a spiritual identity is as much of a mystery as the origin and the creation of man himself. It is not problematical, because it is evident. But it is not transparent, because it is totally caught up in the same transcendence which makes man to be man.

Human affection turns into real love as it discovers

the intimate identity of the human being and reacts accordingly; in other words, as it finds man's lovableness in his irreplaceable selfhood. As it becomes transparent for divine transcendence, this identity at once expands into unsuspected depths of being. Love probes these depths. But we should note that only real love for the other person is perceptive enough to discover these depths and this transcendence in him. Only love brings about the total immersion in the other person which makes such clearsightedness possible. It is the highest kind of "being oneself for the other person," hence the highest degree of receptivity for all that the other person is.

The insight into the transcendent value of the person confers a new dimension upon love. It is no longer a mere relation to one's fellow man as another human being and an indirect relation to the world; it integrates this double relation in God's infinite lovableness. It now becomes a loving of man in God. Thus the highest love for a human person implies an orientation towards God as the ultimate ground of all lovableness. How would a man be able to reach the fellow man he loves in his real being if his love did not penetrate into the very ground of this being; if he did not love him *in the very source* of his lovableness; if the creative originality of the beloved remained hidden;

if the transcendent bond with God's infinity did not fill love with a deeper resonance?

"Loving in God" reveals its whole meaning only when it is understood that the lovableness of the beloved person is not only based upon a sharing of God's own lovableness but is also the presence in man of God's love itself. For, in the final analysis, man is lovable because he is loved by God. This love of God for man is the creative power which not only causes the ability of and the need for real loving in man, it also puts in him the ontological goodness which elicits love. Thus loving one's fellow man is a meeting in him of God's love; and further, some kind of sharing in that love. But divine love is creative and so, at its own level, is every authentic love. It wishes the beloved "to be in himself," it wishes to "make him be," to "cause him to exist" in himself, even as willed by God's love.

The discovery of the divine presence and of the person's originality will remain inchoative as long as it is not reflected in a reciprocal discovery. The awareness that God is man's ultimate cause is perfect only when two human beings together know that God is present in each one of them and when they are aware of this presence as the only ground of their common humanity. In this reciprocal awareness love reaches its highest unification, because it sees itself springing forth from the love from which all love originates.

Although in this "loving in God" we touch the only ground of mutual love, it does not follow that the oppositional structure of the relationship disappears. Even this highest love is not a blending of the two subjects. On the contrary, it allows them fully to unfold their identity and their selfhood. But it implies a complete openness of selfhood, a total receptivity, hence also a reciprocal ontological enrichment. Furthermore, in this "loving in God" rivalry revives, no longer now as a struggle aiming at victory, but as a noble emulation which makes each partner desire to be outstripped by the other in goodness.

An identification or conformity between them is the result of this receptivity and rivalry. But the likeness which arises in this way is seen by each partner as based upon the deeper likeness which both have to God. The similarity created by that love becomes, as the traditional formula used to put it, "a mutual resemblance of subjects in their resemblance to God." What is man's likeness to God if not his personal originality? For man resembles God mainly through the fact that God causes him *to be self* as He is *self,* that God allows him to share his absolute Selfhood. In this way those who love each other experience, in this likeness, their mutual originality as deriving from one

86

and the same Origin, and the unity which arises between them becomes a transcendent unity and association.

There is, however, a considerable difference between the likeness between them and their likeness to God. In the conformity with God the term of the relation is so absolute and so transcendent that it is meaningless to probe for lesser or greater degrees of resemblance. In the mutual relation, on the other hand, this search is full of meaning. Here one can experience both a distinction and a resemblance. In the experience of similarity the experience of a concrete dissimilarity is included. Also, in the reciprocity of equality and conformity the tension of opposites is felt. A certain negative incommunicability is readily apparent which belongs to the essential structure of love, including the "loving in God." But the import of this negativity is not negative. One of its effects is to make the partners see in the original identity of the loved person inexhaustible ontological riches, a treasure which is felt as such precisely because of the impossibility of possessing it completely.

This oppositional structure of the union derives not only from the negative incommunicability of the two individualities but also from the positive incommunicability of the transcendent relation to God. Therefore the relation to one's fellow man can never perfectly integrate the relation to God within itself. However much the two relationships include each other, the communication with the beloved person will never replace the more intimate communication with God. By his very nature man is more at one with God than with himself and with the other human being. And in the living of his life this unity will express itself in a deeper attachment. God is the being of man's being. He is for man Being itself, he is for man All in All. Hence God's lovableness has for man—if he welcomes his being authentically, so that he can see this lovableness—an incomparable power of attraction. That is why man will never be able to confide to another person the ultimate secret of his being. That is God's secret; it is uttered only in the supreme hiddenness and intimacy of his Being. Only the love for God is a perfect giving and receiving. Hence the discretion and reverence which mark all genuine love between human beings: a respect for the right of the beloved to be hidden in God, and union at a high level in the reciprocity of this respect; considerateness in familiarity; a temperate restraint in giving and receiving. Real love is enhanced when it ripens from an initial hesitancy which is a kind of delicate reserve in the expression of a basic desire, and when its shared radiance issues steadily from a depth from which the veil is never wholly lifted.

CHAPTER VII

Ordo Amoris

IN LOVE HUMAN RELATIONS reach their peak; but love has a diversity of forms which we must review, not only on account of this diversity, but also in order to enable us later to define more precisely the specific nature of friendship.

The first form of this diversity is the love of one's neighbor. This is a love for one's fellow man as a neighbor, that is, as living nearby. The expression "living nearby" implies more than a spatial, temporal or biological proximity. If only this material proximity were intended, love of one's neighbor would be restricted to a narrow circle of fellow men. Most people live "far away" from us in that sense. When we say that love of one's neighbor is a love of people who live nearby, the relative clause "who live nearby" has an explicative, not a restrictive meaning: love of one's neighbor is a love of human beings, who, as human beings, *all* live nearby. Hence it extends to all men, without excluding anybody. On the other hand, it is a special form of love, because it loves fellow men *as* neighbors, *as* essentially nearby.

What do we mean when we say that all men are our neighbors, essentially nearby, in close proximity? A further analysis of likeness can answer that question. Nearness and likeness are complementary and convertible ideas. Human beings are similar to one another in nature because all resemble God. They are also different from each other, as they all are different from God. Hence their equality is a matter of likeness, not of identity. In other words, it is a oneness, but a oneness in opposition. Furthermore, likeness expresses only the *ideal* or formal aspect of this oneness. Its *real* aspect might better be called an "approaching."

This approaching or drawing near is another aspect of the same unity as a real event. It is a likeness actually possessed more than it is an intuition; it is a real ontological approximation, an effective "orientation towards" within a "oneness with." Like the resemblance between human beings, this ontological approximation is first and foremost a proximity to God.

But it is also, like the resemblance of human beings to each other, a horizontal movement of approach to one's fellow men. These two moments of essential proximity are once more correlative: human beings are near each other within their common "nearness to God." Thus the whole relationship is a "nearness of human beings to each other in their nearness to God." My fellow man is my neighbor because, along with me, he is near God, and because the same divine presence fills us both.

Therefore love of one's neighbor is in a certain sense the basis of every case of human love. It does not follow that this foundation is known explicitly in the lover's intention in every instance. In formal love of one's neighbor there is such explicit awareness, consequently it is a special form and moment of love.

By its very nature, as we have said, love for one's neighbor embraces *all* men, since it discovers its motive for loving in every one of them. As a mere love of one's neighbor it does not proceed far beyond this general motive. Of course, it is directed towards the *person* of the loved subject, towards his identity and originality, for it is by no means a love for abstract man in general; but it does not yet reach this originality explicitly, and as such. We might say that it is directed towards the person as such, and not yet towards *this person* in particular. Of itself it is not yet characterized by a special selection, as are other forms of love, especially friendship. It is not indifferent towards the concrete person, yet not much attention is given to an intimate progress into the singular identity of the person. This does not in the least mean that love for one's fellow man brings us back to the level of universal benevolence. Nor does it imply a "loving less" than in a love which is more selective. The fact of the matter is rather that it belongs to love of one's neighbor not to know any limits. That is why it is generally love for one's neighbor which enables a man to practice heroic selflessness and to put his life in jeopardy for others.

A further characteristic of love for one's neighbor is that it does not demand love in return. Where there is such love in return, love for one's neighbor will be subsumed under other forms of love, without ceasing to be itself. In such cases it is practiced more or less under the guise of parental love, or conjugal love, or friendship, and so on. But the motive which makes it love for one's neighbor is retained explicitly under these more particular forms. That is why we say that it is merely "subsumed" under them.

In reality, however, even when it evokes no response in the person loved, love for one's neighbor is never deprived of some love in return. For it always finds God in the others, and it knows that God's love always meets it halfway. Loving one's neighbor for the sake of God is far from meaning that we leave out our fellow man. Love for one's neighbor is not a means of loving God, and can never become such a means. This would conflict both with authentic love for God and with true love for man. Man can never serve as a means, not even for loving God, because man is essentially a relation to God. That is why, in the love for one's fellow man, a yearning for some love in return is at work. Its deepest wish is to evoke such a love, because the granting of this love makes the other person intrinsically good, causes him to be authentically himself, integrates him in the ultimate, all-encompassing reality which is the love of men for each other in their shared love for Love itself.

Love for one's neighbor is, as such, not a personal love, although it may become so. It aims at this of its very nature since it reaches its most perfect form as personal love. The fact that love for one's fellow man, which naturally extends to all men—at least in this sense, that it cannot positively exclude anybody—seldom develops into explicit personal love is due to man's limitation. It is humanly impossible to know and love all men personally, owing to the concrete situation of every individual person in the community. Every human being has a relation to the whole community, even to the community of the past and the community of the future. Yet he is connected with it in his own particular way, deriving from his particular existential situation. The multiplicity of men who constitute the community appear in a different light to every individual person, so that this multiplicity assumes a different pattern for each person. As this individual person, a man differs from all the others, and they differ from him. As an individual person he is situated in a community in which all his relations to all other men are of a different kind. Consequently the community as the totality of these relations is never seen in the same light by different people. With some persons a man is intimately, or even very intimately, connected; with others less intimately, with others still less intimately, and so on. The boundaries of his personal concrete community coincide with his conscious contacts. From the nature of this situation arises what St. Thomas calls an "order of charity,"[20] a structure or system of greater or lesser bonds of affection. This order is based upon a twofold principle: a principle of *natural connections,* through which people are united by life itself, and a principle of *free selection,* in which the bonds are the result of a personal preference.

Among the bonds of affection which derive from natural connections belongs first the love for one's parents, or filial love. It is obvious that this attachment of the child to his parents, especially to his mother, cannot from the very start be a wholly conscious and personal love. Initially it is not much more than an instinctive drive for self-preservation. It is the task of psychology to describe the beginnings of this attachment and the various complexes which may develop in these first stages as deviations from normality. It is important to observe that the child's attachment to his parents is born of a need. At first it is what the ancients called a "love of concupiscence" or—to avoid the possible implications of this term—*a love of need*. The attachment to the parents will always be tinged with this "love of need," even after it has grown into a personal love and an explicit *love of benevolence*. It ought to develop in that way, for it belongs to the nature of this affection to rise above the level of outright dependence. It is of the essence of this affection, as Dietrich von Hildebrand remarks, "to pass through certain changes in the different stages of life."[21] Despite these changes, we may speak of a special "type of love," for, although the child does not always remain a child, the adult ever remains the child of his parents.

The passage from childish attachment to authentic filial love will occur mainly through the mediating experience of the parents' love. The gradual transformation from a mere love of need to authentic benevolence will take place because of a growing realization of what the parents mean for the child. Once it has grow into personal love, this attachment will assume such nuances as veneration, fidelity, gratitude, loving remembrance, and so on. Finally the relation may be totally reversed, for there comes a time when the parents need their children's help and when the benevolence into which filial love has developed will have to take care of a real neediness on the part of the parents. This filial love reaches its highest form in a tender solicitude which discreetly anticipates every appeal for help.

This development may pass through some critical stages. For sooner or later life impels the child to throw off his parents' protective love. He must lead his own life, and he must do this by himself. Of course, this development should not break the bonds of affection with the parents. But these bonds will undergo a basic modification. When the child becomes an adult, he stands on a level with his parents, but protective love cannot accept this equality. When the parents do not give up their protective attitude soon enough, it is felt as a guardianship and inevitably evokes some resistance. But even when the parents adapt themselves to the changing situation, their children's affection may be mixed with a slight amount of aggressivity, which might be nothing more than a repercussion of the general aggressivity which the young have to show when they enter into adult life. Hence it frequently happens that during the years of early adulthood love for one's parents, at least as consciously experienced, undergoes a certain decline, which seems to lie in the line of its normal development.

Closely connected with the love for one's parents is the love between brothers and sisters. This love, too, is a special form of affection with characteristics peculiar to it. It is the exercise of a natural existential unity, the result of having been put into life together, the experience of a "we" in its most primitive form. To some extent it lies in the immediate prolongation of love for one's parents, because it is determined by a common descent. Both forms of love include each other: love for one's parents is disturbed by strife among the children, and the mutual attachment of brothers and sisters loses some of its specific identity if it excludes affection for the parents. No wonder, then, if both moments are animated by the same spirit, the spirit peculiar to this particular family, always slightly different from the spirit, the atmosphere and the intimacy of other families, the way individuals differ from each other. This spirit is sometimes very much aware of itself.

Love for one's parents and love for brothers and sisters thus have in common that neither is based on explicit communication. The parents understand the child not because he tells them about his intimate being—of which he himself is hardly aware—but simply because he is *their* child; because, after all, they are themselves, to some extent, this child. On the other hand, the children look to their parents for a protecting love, they look up to them as the guardians of an existence that is not yet sufficiently itself. Their own identity, which they have yet to attain, is still to a great extent safely hidden in their parents.

Neither is mutual affection of brothers and sisters an "opening of the sphere of intimacy."[22] Rather it is the manifestation of an existing solidarity, often animated by a boisterous, although innocuous, rivalry. It is based upon a natural "familiarity,"[23] upon a mutual "being used to each other." This familiarity may, in its turn, lead to intimacy, that is, to the knowledge which siblings have that they can trust each other when the need arises—even to the point of youthful complicity—and that they can confide certain things to each other. But all this does not as yet amount to the sharing of one's most personal intimacy.

The latter element, however, is not excluded. For the mutual attachment of brothers and sisters contains a potentiality for bonds of affection which point to a certain degree of friendship. These bonds generally develop later in life, they give rise to what we may call confidences, which are meant not so much as intimate communications, but rather as a looking for help in concerns and experiences which belong already to the future.

The connection deriving from a natural unity of existence is not limited to the family. The family is not an isolated social phenomenon. It is inserted in a wider circle of family relations, deriving from the kinship to which the parents belonged. But the unity of this wider family bond is much weaker, for the simple reason that it is essentially complex and divided. Thus the children of one family belong to connections on both sides of the family which have not much in common. Moreover, when we consider the family as heading towards the future, we must say that its bonds are loosening. The family in its development averts its face, as it were, from its own unity. All this explains why the emotional ties with relatives who do not belong to the same family—or who once belonged to it, such as married brothers and sisters—do not give rise to special forms of affection. Hence we cannot speak of a typical affection for nephews or nieces. The affection for relatives outside one's immediate family is to a great extent an ordinary human affection. It may find particular motives in kinship; yet, except for some analogy with the fondness of brothers and sisters, this affection is essentially distinguished by no specific properties. It is often characterized by a familiarity like that between brothers and sisters, although the degree of this familiarity will depend on whether or not the feeling of kinship is kept alive by a real living together or by the frequent exchange of visits.

The unity of descent is not limited to the wider bonds of kinship; its ultimate range is, of course, mankind itself. But we have already explained, in connection with love for one's fellow men and personal love, how this universal community of men must take concrete shape in particular manifestations if it is effectively to become the object of affection. One concrete, although very comprehensive, form of this unity through descent is a *people*, or, on a more primitive level, a *tribe*. This unity of a people is very important, not only because it is a unity "to which man belongs essentially, with body, soul and spirit,"[24] but also—and this has great bearing on our problem—because the awareness of belonging to the same people gives rise to an attachment, an affection and even a love with an undeniably specific character.

But what precisely do we mean by a people? It is a social unity, a form of community, which—at least as a people—while not yet implying a juridical organization, is nevertheless determined by a certain number of sociological factors of considerable diversity: biological, geographical, historical, cultural, linguistic, moral, religious, economic, etc. It is well-nigh impossible to enumerate them. And we do not claim that all these factors have the same influence upon the formation of every people, much less that all are equally essential, although the biological unity of descent has a fundamental role. Taken together, these factors constitute that which brings about the formal unity of this people, its character or spirit, in the sense of a characteristic spiritual and psychological mentality which is inherited or inborn. We must further note that whereas these factors constitute the people and its character, they are not, or are to a much lesser extent, required of the individual in order for him to belong to this people. One who has been admitted into a people may, after a lapse of time, really belong to it in spirit or mentality. Second-generation descendants can have a sense of wholly belonging to this people. This phenomenon shows to what extent a people is an objective reality, a peculiar kind of community, existing, of course, only in the individuals who comprise it, yet transcending them as an objective form.

The reality of a people is rooted in a unity of descent, manifests itself in a similarity in the manner of living, in mores and customs, mentality and ideas, but its final expression is a unified *culture*, in which the members of this people see reflected, and possess, their own nature. This explains the supreme importance of *language*—the mother tongue—since nothing constitutes the permanent cultural deposit of a people's specific characteristics to a greater extent than its mother tongue.

This culture, the accumulated wealth produced during many centuries of a people's life, is the precious heritage through which the consciousness of this people endures. Attachment to one's people and love for one's own kindred will always manifest themselves in a pride taken in this inheritance, and, if necessary, in the defense of it. To look upon this inheritance as merely a matter of past glory would imply a wholly erroneous conception of its nature. On the contrary, it is this people's present reality itself; it consists not so much in the material presence of works and institutions, arts and monuments, as in the unity of a common awareness and of the same social spirit and mentality, a unity continually kept in existence by the external objectivity of the culture and developing steadily towards a further destiny.

Yet it is not this *unity as unity* which produces the specific content of a people's consciousness or of one's love for it. The explicit awareness of this unity is what determines the thing called national feeling. For a *nation* is a people which has become aware of itself *as a people*—generally in opposition to other peoples —whereas the *state* is the nation which has worked out its juridical organization completely. As such, the nation is a transition between people and state.

Theoretically the state consisting of only one people would be the ideal. Thus St. Thomas has noted that preferably the state should consist of only one people, because a unity of mores and customs will promote unanimity among the citizens, while states consisting of several peoples have fallen as a result of disunity.[25]

Although theoretically this kind of state is the ideal, we must add that in the course of time the concepts of people and nation have become somewhat relative, though without losing their substantial content. It is partly owing to their relative character that people and nation strive towards the solid form of a state. One more aspect of this relativity is that enormous differences may exist between national groups, nations and peoples. There are peoples and nations with wide geographical extension, others with narrow geographical boundaries. Some live in alliance with others, some are historically, culturally and economically so dependent on others that they have, as it were, grown together with them. Hence it may happen, in our times, that two or more nations are induced to live as one state. On the other hand, certain circumstances may make the scattering of one people over several states acceptable. In all these cases the state should be so organized that the national groups can preserve their identity. This shows that a sound nationalism should not be condemned but is required for the health of a state. For man's attachment to his natural community goes out towards the community of his people and not towards the juridical form in which it is organized.

This attachment remains relative in two ways. First, a people as a cultural group is not hermetically sealed off from other peoples. For wider cultural connections exist between peoples in which one's own cultural heritage is experienced as an element of a wider cultural inheritance. In such cases we speak rather of "cultures," but the term does not matter. Thus Western European culture constitutes a real community to which a man may be attached and which he will preserve and defend as a precious value. Secondly, each individual people allows further particularizations. Such forms of attachment to more local cultural values are sound, provided they do not conflict, like particularism, with the more universal love for and unity of one's people. Love for one's people may be conditioned geographically, in the attachment to one's native soil, to the country, the region—in short, to the natural environment with its inhabitants.

The importance of all these forms of affection is that they constitute the indispensable wider sphere within which the more individual, particular and personal forms of human relations will originate. In many respects they condition the latter, while also constituting the solid ground from which they may develop.

We have not yet spoken of conjugal love because, unlike the previously mentioned relations, this one is not brought about by a natural bond. On the other hand, we cannot simply put it among the forms of affection which are merely based on a free selection, not because such a selection is lacking in conjugal love, but because it is typical of this love to create a *natural bond* as the result of a *free selection*. Yet this love originates in a natural drive which anticipates every selection. Hence conjugal love, while arising from a subjective need, is freely directed to the objective lovableness of the selected person. The subjective need takes its origin from the complementary nature of the sexes, and the objective lovableness makes of the fulfillment of the need a deeply personal relation. It is further typical of conjugal love that this twofold basis of attachment fuses in one undivided experience.

Thus in the conjugal relationship the whole person is involved, spirit and senses. Here sensible attachment becomes translucent for a spiritual—and, as the bond becomes more perfect—for a transcendent personal love, and this love expresses itself in the immediacy of sensible attachment. On account of all this it may be called an adequately human love—that is, a love which in truth is perfectly human, because it has the whole person as its subject and as its object.

Perfectly human does not necessarily mean humanly perfect. The fact that in the union of man and woman affection finds its adequately human form does not yet mean that—owing only to this form—this affection is the loftiest kind of human love. But it may grow into such an ideal form of love. Conjugal love too finds its purest authenticity when it becomes a "loving in God," and it is an error to think that its specific form and deeply human character constitute an obstacle to this "loving in God," or that they would have to be renounced for conjugal love to discover as transcendent the lovableness which gave rise to it.

Conjugal love finds its spontaneous expression and exercise in the marriage act. Therefore it belongs to the essence of this act that it be performed in real love for the other person. Such a love is real only when it is exclusive, because, by its very nature, it involves the whole human being, within the sexual complementarity of individual persons. The sexual act has no acceptable meaning if it is not the expression of a unique personal love.

This act is not the only expression of the marriage partners' affection. Rather, it is one moment of a much wider living together in which both manifest their love by making every effort to render each other happy. Thus marriage is a real community of life.

Furthermore, there is a temporal development in conjugal love which, when it is authentic, will lead to an ever more intimate union. The first moment of it is the discovery of the affection itself, the realization of its prospects and of its possible endurance. This moment corresponds to *being in love*. Being in love is already a real beginning of love, although in a rather potential way. Essentially it is only an experiencing of love as potentiality, as future possibility.

It is already turned towards a definite person, although the choice is not final, even if the lovers have the opposite impression and feel that there can be no more doubt about the final selection. Whereas authentic love may be called clearsighted—the proverbial blindness of love is an attribute of infatuation —it is difficult to say the same for the initial "being in love."

Being in love is a still undifferentiated moment of love. This is closely connected with its potential character and almost coincides with it. The aspect of undifferentiation adds something to that of potentiality: a relative aspect to the awareness of affection because of the experience of an internal opposition. This relative character—let us not forget it—belongs to the concrete exercise of every awareness which reaches the level of reality. This awareness of reality, however, is not the most typical feature of being in love. That is not because it takes the unreal as its object, but rather because no clear distinction is made between reality and unreality, since it is mainly the *unlimited possibility* of loving with which consciousness is filled. Absence of limits and potentiality are completely correlative aspects in the present instance. The possibility may look like an unlimited vista, because it is as yet no more than a possibility; on the other hand, the absence of limits is only that of a possibility. For clearness' sake we must add that we are speaking of a possibility in the strict sense of that word, hence the fact of not yet being realized does not cloud the outlook on future possibilities. It enters consciousness only by way of desire, and this desire again is experienced in a positive way.

We might almost say that being in love is the esthetic initial moment of love. We call *esthetic* the manifestation of some absolute in a concrete visible form. In the present case the lovers themselves constitute this form, and the absolute which takes shape in them is the unlimited perspective of their mutual lovableness as the object of an unrestricted possibility of loving. No wonder, then, if people who are in love find each other handsome, beautiful and lovable, and experience their affection as a *beautiful* love. That beauty possesses evidence unique for them, which is closely tied to their particular situation and as a result does not present itself to persons outside this situation.

While we may call the phenomenon of being in love considered as an objective contemplation esthetic, as a subjective experience of companionship and familiarity, of living and talking together, it assumes rather the form of playing—which is likewise true of the subjective experience of any esthetic activity. This playing is—barring the intrusion on this mood of a prematurely aroused passion—a playing with possibilities. As such we might consider it (some philosophical theories of play notwithstanding) as in some way a prelude to life; to that life which, while not necessarily "expelling the first joy," will no longer consist of mere playing.

But every prelude reaches an end, whether it is arrested in failure or reaches its natural fulfillment. This fulfillment begins with the final choice of the partner. Possibility has now become reality. But this reality turns out to be a gradual and relative realization. The "illusion" that the complete mutual donation would at once reach its total fruition as a result of the final choice must yield to the insight that it can be carried out only through a whole life. This insight includes the revelation that authentic love is more serious than its esthetic prelude intimated, because the prelude contained no awareness of all that the reality of life would entail in the way of cares and worries, uncertainty and sacrifice, difficulties arising from the psychic dispositions of the partners themselves. But authentic love is nourished by this rather than hindered by it, especially since the partners slowly come to a fuller realization that the donation of oneself can turn into a real donation only through living and experiencing the fullness of concrete life. Neither do the limitations of the partners as individuals—limitations which will necessarily show up in many spheres—mean a decrease in the lovableness each has for the other; rather, this will mean a deepening of the reality in which this lovableness, too, becomes real.

Hence it is not true that the initial esthetic absoluteness which filled the atmosphere of "being in love" vanishes in real love, to be replaced by a reality of a very different appearance. We should say, on the contrary, that the experience of this absoluteness with all its vistas will be perpetuated in real love—in proportion to its authenticity—no longer as the potential totality of the relationship, but as a *particular moment*. This moment, which may be considered as a constitutive factor of conjugal love, may be called the *erotic moment*. The term "erotic" has been scientifically and unscientifically used in so many senses and abused in so many ways in modern times that it is worth our while to restore its authentic meaning. The erotic is the essentially contemplative aspect of love, through which love sees itself as absolute value in the lovableness of the loved one as concretely embodied. It is the delightful intuitive possession of the full possibilities of love, unaccompanied by the awareness that these possibilities are not yet wholly actualized. In its erotic aspect actual love coincides with its unlimited perspectives. In other words, it is a permanent "being in love," but within the communion of the partners itself, the embodied gratuitousness of love, by which it is a loving for loving's sake, a loving pure and simple. It bestows upon human love its perfect human delight.

The mistake of some modern conceptions is practically to deny the spiritual meaning of the erotic aspect, thus equating it simply with sexual passion, whereas it is precisely erotism which gives this passion its human meaning. Passion too, as translated in the body, is a moment of conjugal love, since this love involves the whole of man. In its esthetic, eventually in its idyllic, beginnings these two moments were not yet differentiated. For being in love means experiencing love as an unlimited, but also as an undetermined, potentiality. Such experiencing of potentiality is of its nature undifferentiated, the experience of some undefined "all and nothing." As soon as actual love begins, its real structure asserts and shows itself; that is, the various moments contained within it, which at first were not distinct, emerge into consciousness in clearer contrast. This means that conjugal love will be felt as a duality of contrary aspects: on the one hand, it is experienced as a spiritual self-donation to the beloved person, a supreme *love of benevolence*, expressing itself in a great and effective tenderness and in a unique generosity, ready for all sacrifices in order to make one another happy; on the other hand, it is an attachment born of a need, a *love of concupiscence*, which enjoys the proffered affection as a subjective satisfaction.

The fact that these two moments show an internal opposition derives not from love itself, nor from its actualization, but from its imperfection, which explains why love's constitutive moments have not yet reached their total meaning. That is why they are felt as opposed to each other. This opposition is transcended in proportion as both of them become that which essentially they tend to become: a personal donation, in which the bodily experience is nothing but the pure expression of a love totally animated by the objective lovableness. How much this perfection of love is conditioned by the increasing realization of the transcendent bond between the beloved and God needs no further comment after what we said above. But we must emphasize that it is wrong to believe that the specific form by which conjugal love differs from other forms of love might be an obstacle to this realization. Such a belief proceeds from a false conception of this love itself; it overlooks the fact that such love, too, enables man to renounce himself. In its very fulfillment love points to such a renunciation.

Conjugal love is a mutual donation which includes the whole person. In this donation what is given is not lost; on the contrary, it issues from the giving itself. For the famous saying that nobody can give what he does not possess (*nemo dat quod non habet*) is true only insofar as it is corrected by the opposite assertion, that nobody possesses what he does not share with others (*nemo habet nisi quod dat*). Love's donation is reciprocal, and this reciprocity too is a constitutive element in this sense, that the two donations, in their perfect meeting, are exalted into a single donation, by which the same reality is given and received and by which both acquire, in this unity, an independence which transcends their twofold reality. The double donation of the person as person rediscovers itself in the unity of a third person, the child. Considered from the standpoint of their mutual love, the child is primarily the very love which man and woman feel for each other. The child is this love in perfect human embodiment, it is the objective reality and final actuality of the vital donation they have made to each other.

In the undivided selfhood of the child the partners behold and experience their mutual unity as a personified achievement. In the children their love beholds its lifegiving wealth. If we remember that human love is a "being oneself for others," we shall not be surprised that a love which wholly assumes this "being oneself," together with a complete "mutually being for each other," culminates in the production of a real selfhood. This shows how essentially the children are the fruit of love, and how totally the meaning of the child is misunderstood when it is considered as merely the biological—eventually undesired—result of the marriage act; but also how conjugal love is maimed in its nature and disintegrates into a twofold egoism, held together merely by subjective pleasure, when the child is simply and intentionally excluded.

Thus conjugal love discovers its complement and its completion in the love for the children. Now the partners love each other not only as husband and wife but also as father and mother of the children. The children are the final embodiment of the mutual love. Yet the child remains a third person; this explains why the love of the parents for the child has peculiarities which distinguish it from their mutual love. To the parents' love corresponds the child's love for the parents. Yet this is no reciprocal love in the full meaning of the word. For the two forms of love are quite different, nor can they be interpreted exclusively as responses to each other. One cannot even say that both forms of love *directly* intend a love in return. The parents see in the child the unity of their reciprocal love. In the child they love the very reality of their love for each other. But this reality, as Hegel says, is "object" and "substantial being"; it has become "an existence which is for itself."[26] In the child the love of the parents for each other has stepped outside itself as an independent objectivity; their love, quite naturally, is drawn by this objectivation. Hence the parents love the child in its own being, because the bestowing of that own being is precisely their love. In this sense the love for the children means a deepening of mutual affection, because this affection develops into a *giving* which really transcends the *receiving*. Mutual love is exalted into a love which already includes a giving up of that which is loved. The parents love the child, as Dietrich von Hildebrand says, as turned towards its own life and its own future career.[27] They do not want to take the child back for themselves. They love it, but they do not wish to appropriate it. The parents—herein lies the great selflessness of their donation—love the child, as it were, *away from themselves,* they love it towards its own future and independence. This independence will sooner or later entail the children's leaving father and mother because some other love invites them.

As for the child, it *is* this independence. True, it is likewise substantially the mutual communication and love of the parents, but it is such *unconsciously*. It can never realize what it means for its parents. Therefore the children's love never equals the love the parents have for them. It cannot be otherwise, it has to be this way. Thus Hegel remarks that "as a whole, the children love the parents less than the parents love the children, for they are heading for independence, they grow stronger, hence they leave their parents behind them."[28] It is true that the parents "possess permanently in the children the objective objectivation of their union,"[29] but the very objectivity of this *objectivation,* its solid reality, is based upon a renunciation in which the mutual love is raised to a higher plane of goodness. Once they have reached autonomy, the children move away from their parents, who keep the joy of their children's attachment only as a remembrance, a remembrance which, like their mutual love and their love for their children, remains the personal and incommunicable secret of the parents alone.

The arrival and departure of the children will bring conjugal love to its spiritual maturity. This love underwent a first change when it suddenly assumed the form of loving each other as father and mother of the child. In caring for and working for the growing children, it became the ruling principle of the small realm of the family, which prospered in the joy of a many-sided affection. By giving up the children for their own sake, selfless love reaches its completion. This completion means love deepened and spiritualized into conjugal friendship, at times recovering a "being in love" which has now grown to full maturity. This is its evening splendor. Like every human love, conjugal love too will have known the ups and downs of happy and sad circumstances; but both will have carried this love to its highest—perhaps transcendent—reality, because it might well be that both are required for the expression and the actualization of authentic human love.

CHAPTER VIII

Friendship

THUS FAR WE HAVE SAID almost nothing about one form of human love: *friendship*. The reason is not, of course, that friendship would find no place in the "order of love," but rather that it is not so easy to determine this place exactly. Hence it was preferable to defer this attempt until we were able to compare with friendship the other forms of human love. There is always the danger of our being satisfied with a vague description in which the proper character of friendship never comes into its own. The *"philia"* of Aristotle and the *"amor amicitiae"* of St. Thomas have not quite avoided this pitfall.

We may begin by admitting that friendship does not

arise from a previous natural connection, as, for instance, does the affection of brothers and sisters. This does not mean that the latter may not assume some of the features of friendship. Neither can we say that friendship derives from a true *need*. When Aristotle calls it *"anagkaiotaton"* (something quite indispensable),[30] he seems to derive the necessity not so much from a subjective need as from the high value of friendship. "For nobody would wish to live without friends, even if he possessed all other good things."[31] Hence the principle of friendship is undoubtedly a free selection. But this selection does not give rise to a natural bond, as in married love. Friendship rather perpetuates the free selection as such. It is an affection which continues to arise from freedom and knows no other necessity than this freedom itself. It is essentially the most *free love* there is. It can come to an end at any time, since nothing hinders such a termination. But it will not cease, because it does not wish to. That is why freedom does not make friendship an unstable relationship. For although its motive is freely accepted, its intrinsic value and the fact that it is established spontaneously and freely guarantee the durability of the affection. This does not prevent some friendships from dying, for even friendship does not necessarily escape the fundamental relativity of everything human. Since friendship is perhaps the most clearsighted of all forms of love, it may be that it will find in the very awareness of this human frailty a weapon against it. Finally, friendship is, of course, a form of personal affection; in being personal it rises above the non-selectiveness of love for one's neighbor, though not above the latter's transcendent character. What evokes friendship is the spiritual attractiveness radiating from the deepest nature of the other.

Since friendship is a personal love resulting from a free choice, the question naturally arises: Why does *this* person make *that* person his friend? Does this happen arbitrarily, do some predispositions influence the choice, or is the beginning of a friendship merely a lucky accident? Perhaps none of these possibilities is to be excluded, and we might find the explanation where the three converge. First, a lucky chance may be involved. Does not every encounter have an element of luck? Can we call a planned encounter a real encounter? The interesting, beautiful, splendid aspect of an encounter is its character of surprise, of unexpected and sudden discovery. Albrecht Goes writes, "In reality, nobody can do anything to make a friendship begin. Its origin depends on the gratuitous grace of encounter."[32] Of course, in such an encounter we must see much more than a purely material "happening upon" or "coming across." Thus it is quite possible that we have never "encountered" a person we

have come across dozens of times, even talked with occasionally. These encounters—if we want to call them
that—happened without invitation, there was no authentic human interest, not much curiosity, no desire
to linger, no surprise, no spiritual insight. That is why
in the end two such persons have passed each other by
without any feeling of separation and without any
great desire of seeing each other again. But then "suddenly a look of joy wells up, a luminous mutual understanding." The conversation which ensues is quite
ordinary, yet it is "like music of the heart, like a so-
nata by Mozart, full of harmony."[33]

Every friendship depends on such a chance, it can
never be planned in advance. It is a surprise gift, a
"gratuitous grace of encounter." But this chance is not
some kind of external situation which automatically
determines the birth of the friendship. This would
contradict one of its most essential characteristics,
namely that it springs forth from the spirit's free
spontaneity. From its very beginning it is marked by
complete gratuitousness. Choosing somebody as a
friend is dictated by no reason and falls within no
obligation. The choice may be made or not made. It
is made only because both have so decided. The chance
may then be called a double chance in this sense, that
both freely and spontaneously will the same thing.
The surprise can come only as a mutual surprise, due

to a lucky chance. And this surprise itself consists in the sudden evidence of a perfect reciprocity.

The question then arises whether this reciprocity is the result of a previous attunement of mind and heart. Aristotle put the question in a slightly different way, which amounts to the same thing: Is friendship based upon an existing similarity or upon some special kind of dissimilarity? Is it the discovery of an essential agreement or is the agreement of friendship the result of the harmonious complementarity of two opposites?[34] We answer the question by rejecting the either-or. It is obvious that every friendship rests upon some similarity, some mutual consonance. How could unity arise between two persons if they did not possess the aptitude for this unity? But it would be premature to conclude that friendship is nothing but the manifestation of such aptitude, than the consecration of an unconsciously pre-existing understanding. Excluding every kind of opposition would rob friendship of a great deal of its riches. If even man's self-consciousness, as explained in the beginning of this book, is not a tautology, unification with another self-consciousness is much less so.

Friendship is the altogether free and independent communication of one's own person; that is, of the deepest nature of man, which reveals itself both as wholly new, because of its inalienable selfhood, and as

wholly different, because of its individuality. It gives
the two friends access to the unique world constructed
by their spirit. And this unique character is even more
pronounced and more surprising because friendship
does not depend on a natural bond, which tends to
make the partners more alike. Therefore, to a greater
extent than in other human relations, contrast is essential in friendship. And the exceptional enrichment
of life which it brings about derives largely from these
individual and personal oppositions. Friendship can
tolerate wide differences in views and opinions, knowledge and ability, preferences and prejudices, temperament and character, age and social position. The mar-
vel is how it can reconcile all these differences in one
single affection, and how it allows all of them to work
towards greater unity. In practice no friendship will
live without friendly disagreements. They belong to
the fabric of the relationship. It is precisely the
strength of a friendship that it can tolerate all this
without danger to its unity.

The bond created by friendship is not a material
equality in thought and feeling, it is rather the actualization of an equal quality of the spirit, of a shared
appreciation for human spiritual values. Friends are
persons of the same caliber, on the same spiritual
level. From what we have said before of love's transcendence, it is evident that this quality of the spirit

will be more substantial in proportion as it derives from a deeper realization of man's origin and destiny.

The transcendent range of love will emerge more easily in friendship, because true friendship is mainly a spiritual bond. A community of material interests does not yet create a friendship. Friends will do anything to render each other a service, but the reciprocity of these services is no motive for friendship. Friendship, as a special form of affection, stands outside the sphere of the sexual, hence also of the erotic. Yet the relation of friendship shows some analogy with the erotic moment of love. First because both suppose an accidental and lucky encounter. Next, in both of them affection is clearly gratuitous, granted for affection's sake; but whereas in erotism this gratuitousness passes gradually into a natural connection, in friendship it endures as a permanent feature. The relation of friendship maintains its freedom and independence, its bonds arise immediately from this freedom. In friendship we also meet the typically esthetic aspects of erotism, but with an essential difference. In erotism the fusion between spiritual affection and its manifestation in body and senses is so intimate that spiritual affection is experienced as being identical with bodily attraction. In the relationship of friendship, on the other hand, the bodily appearance becomes the free expression of a drawing nearer of the spiritual person as such; it is not a vague and bodily exaltation, but a formal "splendor of goodness" and an embodiment of benevolence. In short, while erotism is like a beautiful ruse of adequate human love, leading this love by very subjective roads towards its objective purpose, friendship remains an exceptional luxury in human relations by which human beings join together spiritually in complete liberty.

Yet we may not conclude from the absence of the principle of need that the love of friendship is less durable than other forms of love which are directly or indirectly determined by some need. Of course, the physical necessity connected with helplessness and with bonds arising from nature is lacking. The bond friendship establishes can always be severed; it is precisely in the fact of its not being severed, despite the ever present possibility, that the peculiar faithfulness so typical of authentic friendship consists. Yet this faithfulness, too, derives its whole meaning from friendship itself, without the support of extrinsic motives. It *is* friendship itself, insofar as friendship is "forever." It is "forever" by its very nature and not through some extrinsic quality, although this "being forever" has no other foundation than the free will of each friend.

It is already evident that fidelity to friendship is by no means some kind of automatism. On the contrary, this fidelity will continually have to bear witness to itself by admitting quite a number of things which threaten it more or less. For, like all human things, a relation of friendship does not run an even course. The set of oppositions which it brings together can sometimes reach a point of rather high tension; a change of circumstances, burdens and worries may distract the friend's attention or make the tokens of friendship so rare that it looks as if he were neglecting us. The differences of temperament may be wider than was suspected at first, misunderstandings may arise, and offenses against the friendship are not excluded. Throughout all this, in a relation of friendship which has gone deep enough to deserve the name of authentic friendship, belief in the once experienced evidence of reciprocal affection will continue to be preserved. This fidelity helps it to recover, and in the end fidelity finds a way to make all the contingencies which have threatened it the means of greater unity. The mutual experience of human relativity can lead to a better realization of the value of friendship, can induce the friends to build their affection on more solid ground. A friendship which is to last very soon ceases to be romantic. Feeling turns into insight. If affection grows apace with the insight, it will be able to surmount, by the spontaneity of its free goodness, the human limitations of the friend, which do not escape its clearsightedness, to integrate these limitations in his objective lovableness, because it realizes—from its own experience—how human goodness is always mixed with frailty, but how, on the other hand, this very frailty has its value, because it belongs to the concrete condition of goodness. In this way real friends are led to like each other not *despite* their human defects but simply *with* their defects because these defects happen to be the friend's defects and are part of him. Friendship has this in common with human life, that we get to know its nature only through experience, and that this experience loses no time in doing away with idyllic appearances in order to discover the deeper human values.

If the origin of friendship is a matter of chance, its preservation is not. "If little or nothing can be done to make a friendship begin, much has to be done to keep it alive."[35] Yet whatever can be done can occur only within the complete liberty and independence which happen to be the very essence of friendship. In the domain of friendship nothing can be extorted. As a result friendship does not know the nagging worry about itself which is sometimes experienced in other forms of love, especially when a threat to their existence is felt. It is not even in its line to grieve too much when circumstances weaken or destroy it, although this does not mean that its memory will be lost in indifference.

Furthermore, it follows from this freedom that the mutual affection involved is not the theme of the relation of friendship. Friends do not speak of their feelings of affection the way, for instance, lovers do. They simply stand together in the reality of life. This reality keeps them steadily occupied, and they experience their profound understanding in function of this reality. Hence engaging in friendship is more than anything else an agreeable intercourse and a happy companionship. That is why friendship is capable of spreading its splendor over a whole life. But the source of this splendor remains itself unseen. It is visible only in its radiation, and this radiation takes shape in unexpected attentions, in a spontaneous sharing of weal and woe, and in the absence of all fear about bothering one another. Explicit declarations of affection are superfluous.

When we recall the properties and the high demands of authentic friendship and reflect, further, that there must be a lucky chance to bring people together in friendship, we begin to suspect that authentic friendship is rarer than might be supposed. In this light, Aristotle's concept of *"poluphilia"* (many-friendedness)[36] looks rather dubious. Especially since we must carefully distinguish this authentic friendship from a number of relations which look somewhat like friendship on the surface but lack almost everything belonging to its nature: comradeship, collegiality, fellowship, conviviality, fraternization, association, familiarity, and so on. This is true in particular of the so-called friendliness—*"affabilitas"*—of St. Thomas,[37] which has very real value for peaceful coexistence but consists mainly in external formalities and shows only a remote resemblance to the cordiality of friendship.

Furthermore, one can have comradeship, familiarity, and so on, with several people at the same time. People in company out of sociability naturally expect a wider group, and one can be friendly with almost everybody. Friendliness can serve as a mask even for the most negative feelings. On the other hand, it is doubtful whether one can be a *friend* to several people simultaneously. This does not mean that we cannot have several friends. That is, of course, quite possible. But the question is whether they share one and the same friendship, whether there can really be an authentic "group of friends" in which all are directly united through one bond of friendship. This seems impossible. The different relations of friendship are so personal that they have only one friend as their object. It is possible that these relations, whose number will always be very small, are such that a few people are friends with each other. *A* may be the friend of *B*, *B* of *C* and *C* of *A,* and these various relations may be known by all the others and even considered as almost equivalent. This is a case of comradeship in friendship.

Authentic friendship of a high order calls for an uncommon endowment in mind and in heart, a rich endowment but one which may make a man vulnerable, too; it culminates in a free openness and liberality of the person's whole being. Such a friendship is made possible by what one might call a feeling for friendship. For there is a feeling for friendship as there is a feeling for art, for poetry, for organization, and so on. This feeling is a special power of empathy for all that concerns the object of the feeling; it is also a special power of discernment permitting one to distinguish, even in the most obscure borderline cases, what is authentic from what is not. It is an insight into the nature of things, a realization of their extraordinary value, and an ability to express oneself graciously and spontaneously in words and actions. Above all, having a feeling for something implies that one likes, finds pleasure in, exercising this feeling for its own sake. Thus there are people who have a feeling for friendship, "who love to love." Others lack this feeling, as they may lack a feeling for music, for nature, and even for truth. Or at least such a feeling remains rudimentary. Such a lack consists simply in "not seeing"; it is like the absence of a sense, but it is not recognized as an absence, for the awareness of the absence would presuppose the presence of the feeling.

The feeling for friendship shows a strong analogy with the feeling for happiness; to a great extent, the two coincide. The feeling for happiness also is a special aptitude for being happy, the capacity for finding the source of happiness everywhere, even in the minutest events of life; especially the disposition for putting happiness above all else. Strange as it may sound, that feeling, too, is lacking in many people. They have a feeling for fun, for pleasure, for the satisfaction found in wealth and power, but they have no real capacity for simply feeling happy on account of their happiness itself.

The connection between friendship and happiness consists in the fact that "being happy" means essentially, "being happy with." Happiness as a merely individual possession will soon fade for want of the "reflection" whereby the person sees his happiness reflected in the happiness of another person. But this reflection is not mere *knowledge*. It is a *bringing about* of the mutual happiness by mutual communication. Especially in the sphere of happiness a man really possesses only what he gives to others. This is true in all the forms of personal love, but in friendship most particularly.

But friendship is not exempt from the relative character of everything human. However undivided, sincere and faithful it may be, it is bound to discover in itself a certain inability to give itself to the limit. Thus in friendship, too, there revives—more intensely in proportion as the friendship is deeper—the fundamental loneliness of man as man. Yet in this existential loneliness, the awareness of the bond of friendship is both strong and strengthening, and undoubtedly the common reflection of the mutual solitude itself lightens the burden of this solitude, although it would be an illusion to expect that it might ever completely free man of his loneliness. The reason for this is that man's deepest loneliness derives from the transcendence of his nature. This nature is ultimately a "loneliness for God." That is why it also has a positive meaning. As "loneliness for" it turns into an *expecting* and an *abiding*, a hopeful looking for something great that is to come. This positive aspect of loneliness too is shared in love and friendship, it can be held in common because it is something positive. Expecting becomes expecting together. In this expecting together human love and friendship fulfill their ultimate potentiality.

In the light of this perspective the event which seems to break up the friendship, the death of one of the friends, becomes as it were a consecration of this friendship. One of them at least has now overcome loneliness, even though this may make the loneliness of the surviving friend more oppressive. Yet over this loneliness is diffused a gentle light, emanating from a deeper knowledge that for one of them the great communion has begun. He has led the way. And he remains invisibly present to his friend, he awaits him, knowing that before long both of them will be joined again in a friendship which is forever.

· Notes ·

1. Hegel, *The Phenomenology of Mind*, translated by J. B. Baillie (New York, Macmillan, 2d ed., 1949), p. 219.
2. *Ibid.*, p. 219.
3. *Ibid.*, p. 229.
4. *Ibid.*, p. 230.
5. *Ibid.*, p. 230.
6. *Ibid.*, p. 231.
7. A. Hesnard, *Psychanalyse du lien interhumain* (Paris, 1957), pp. 15f.
8. *Ibid.*, p. 45.
9. Hegel, *op. cit.*, p. 231.
10. A. Hesnard, *op. cit.*, p. 25.
11. *Ibid.*, p. 28.
12. *Ibid.*, p. 28.
13. *Ibid.*, p. 28.
14. L. Vander Kerken, S.J., *De goede mens en zijn gebreken* (Antwerp, 1957), pp. 187f.

141

15. A Hesnard, *op. cit.*, p. 74.

16. Hegel, *op. cit.*, p. 231.

17. *Ibid.*, p. 220.

18. *Ibid.*, p. 233.

19. *Ibid.*, p. 160.

20. St. Thomas, *Summa Theologica*, II–II, q. 26.

21. Dietrich von Hildebrand, *Metaphysik der Gemeinschaft* (Augsburg, 1930), p. 61.

22. *Ibid.*, p. 68.

23. *Ibid.*, p. 67.

24. Theodor Steinbüchel, *Die philosophische Grundlegung der katholischen Sittenlehre* (Düsseldorf, 1951, Vol. 1, 2. Halbband), p. 179.

25. St. Thomas, *In Aristotelis Politica*, Bk. III, lect. 2.

26. Hegel, *Grundlinien der Philosophie des Rechts*, No. 173.

27. Dietrich von Hildebrand, *op. cit.*, p. 58.

28. Hegel, *op. cit.*, No. 175, Zusatz.

29. *Ibid.*, No. 175, Zusatz.

30. Aristotle, *Nicomachean Ethics*, Bk. VIII. ch. 1.

31. *Ibid.*, Bk. VIII, ch. 1.

32. Albrecht Goes, *Von Mensch zu Mensch* (Frankfort on the Main), 1953, p. 127.

33. *Ibid.*, p. 128.

34. Aristotle, *op. cit.*, Bk. VIII, ch. 1.

35. Albrecht Goes, *op. cit.*, p. 128.

36. Aristotle, *op. cit.*, Bk. VIII, ch. 1.

37. St. Thomas, *Summa Theologica*, II–II, q. 114.